AUTOBIOGRAPHY OF AN AWAKENING

◆

ANDREW COHEN

Moksha Foundation
1992

C O N T E N T S

INTRODUCTION

How does one introduce the story of another man's victory over the world? For that is what this is. It is the story of a man who has, with his whole being, won the prize that most people, in their entire life, will only glimpse for a flickering moment. It is the story of a man who gave himself totally to that flicker, and whose passion for Truth has become a hurricane.

It is indeed a difficult story to introduce. But not only because it is so unheard of and so explosive in what it forces the heart to consider, but also because it is a story that can have no closure, no end, no safe limits – a story that any true seeker must eventually enter.

Said most simply, *Autobiography of an Awakening* is the concise story of Andrew Cohen's search for the Truth, his arrival at the end of that searching (in the meeting of his teacher), and his awe-inspiring exploration into the true nature of Enlightenment.

The account is riveting. And my own joy in reading it comes not only from the purity, integrity, and Grace that is revealed here, but from my own direct knowledge that in Andrew Cohen these are not passing phenomena, but are the sparkling facets of a permanent absolute condition that has set Andrew apart from every other person that I have ever met.

When I first saw Andrew enter the satsang room in Corte Madera, California in November 1989, I remember the shock of recognition at the instant my eyes fell upon him. I knew immediately, and without a doubt, that here was a man who had crossed over. Here was a man who somehow embodied an experience that I had had twelve years earlier, and which had haunted me since. In that instant, a sense of drift that had characterized my life for years, suddenly was corrected.

I watched Andrew like a hawk – every word, gesture and glance. I didn't know how I was seeing what I saw, for other than his eyes, there was no single quality or characteristic that set him apart from other people. Yet somehow, it was plainly there. The question that had plagued me for years – is it really possible to *live* the truth? – had found a living answer.

Since that night, I have seen Andrew teach hundreds of times in countlessly varied situations. And in all of his answers to all of the thousands of questions that people have asked him, there has been only the relentless dance of an absolute clarity, and an unquenchable thirst for the destruction of ignorance. No stone is left unshattered. No matter the source of the question, Andrew's answers lead always and only to one place. And as often as I have seen him teach, I've marveled at the paradox of his infinite, palpable sameness, expressed in infinite, thrilling variety.

But equally compelling as the Truth which roars in Andrew and his teaching, is the utter impeccability that manifests itself in every aspect of his life. The effect of this perfect cohesion on so many people has been staggering to witness. For there is a trust and clarity that blooms in and between those around him which is truly rare. All is open to inquiry, and nothing is hidden.

If I could do one simple thing in the introduction of this triumphant story, it would simply be to tell you, the reader, that it really is true. That the awesome possibilities raised here – those that your heart almost dares not to believe – are *exactly* what has happened. It may seem too fantastic for this world, and what can one say? For it does seem that it could have no place here, and yet here it is.

Jeff Bitzer

This is the story of my life. I felt it had to be written because I know there are many people who have been through similar trials in the search for themselves. Anybody who sincerely seeks for Liberation will be severely tested. I encourage that individual who truly wants to be Free to stand alone in the Truth, as I have been forced to do. There is no other way.

Andrew Cohen
December 26, 1991

CHILDHOOD

1

I was born in New York City on October 23, 1955.
Except for brief moments my childhood was an
unhappy one. My parents did not love each other
and my older brother of five years was very resentful
of my presence in his life. By the time I was five years
old, it was noted that something was wrong, because
even though it was obvious that I was a bright child
in elementary school, I was unable to absorb much of
what was being taught. Because of this, my mother,
who had been by that time very involved with psychoanalysis herself for many years, sent me to a child
psychologist. I continued to go to this psychologist for
the next ten years. My identity throughout my entire
childhood and early adolescence was that I had a
"problem." In spite of the psychoanalysis and the fact
that I was in a progressive elementary school, my
inability to absorb information the way many of my
classmates seemed to be able to continued to convince
me that something was very wrong. At the time I was
approximately eight or nine years old, the psychoana-
lyst had me lie down on a couch in the traditional
manner and encouraged me to free-associate – which
meant I was to try to verbalize freely and without
censorship any and all thoughts and feelings that
arose.

As a result of seeing the Beatles perform on "The Ed Sullivan Show" and the general mood of the time, I became interested in music and decided that I wanted to play the drums. When I was eleven, my mother told me that she was going to separate from my father. Some time later, she left New York to go live in Italy. I remained in New York and continued to live with my father and brother. When I was thirteen, my father, after experiencing many severe headaches, discovered that he had a brain tumor. Shortly after that, he had surgery and I was informed that he had only a year to live. When I was fourteen years old, I left the progressive elementary school I had attended for seven years and entered a private high school for students with learning problems. Shortly after entering high school, I began to experiment with drugs, as many people were in those days. There I made some very close friends and we spent much of our time playing rock 'n' roll music together in the basement of my friend's house in Greenwich Village. From the thrill of making music together and the intimacy and respect for each other that we shared, we experienced many moments of joy.

My father died shortly after my fifteenth birthday. My mother, who was aware of the fact that I was experimenting with drugs, worried about this and informed me that I would be going to a progressive boarding school in Switzerland. Despairing at leaving my new friends and the joy of playing music together, reluctantly I left for Switzerland. Arriving there, I felt very out of place because by that time I was fully identified with being a young hippie and found the discipline and confinement suffocating. After a year, I was kicked out for smoking marijuana. I went to live with my mother in Rome where I immediately enrolled in another small progressive school. The almost two years that I spent there were happy ones and a time of learning for me. For the first time in my life, I started reading, and because of the unusual new school I was in, one of my teachers had me reading Freud, Jung and R.D. Laing. These studies were quite extraordinary and inspired me a great deal. While in Rome, I met some local musicians and began to play avant-garde jazz with them.

When I was sixteen years old, the most extraordinary thing happened to me. Late one night as I was talking with my mother, for no apparent reason I began to experience a completely new and unimaginable condition. My consciousness began to expand in all directions simultaneously and I experienced what could only be called revelation. Tears profusely poured out of my eyes and my throat repeatedly opened and closed for no reason. I was feeling completely overwhelmed and intoxicated by Love and was struck by a sense of awe and wonder that is impossible to describe. I suddenly knew without any doubt that there was no such thing as death and that life itself had no beginning and no end. I saw that all of life was intimately connected and inseparable. It became clear that there was no such thing as individuality separate from that one Self that was all of life. The glory and majesty in the cosmic unity that was revealing itself to me was completely over-whelming. I could hardly speak. My mother told me years later that I had said to her at the time not to worry, that I was not unhappy, and that this used to happen to me often when I was a child. In the midst of this explosion I was struck by what seemed to be a message that came directly from the revelation itself. That message was: if you give your life to me *alone* you have nothing to fear. Disoriented, it took me several days to recover from the impact that this explosion had on my mind and body.

No one who I described this extraordinary event to seemed able to appreciate its significance or even understand what I was talking about. Fortunately the unusual teacher who had given me Freud and Jung to read had also given me *The Varieties of Religious Experience* by William James, which helped to give me some understanding of what had just occurred.

Still fervently interested in becoming a jazz musician, I was accepted at the Berklee College of Music in Boston and went there to enter the fall semester at the end of my seventeenth year. I had a very difficult time almost immediately because I had little formal training and could not even read music. Because of this, I decided to leave at the end of the first semester and entered a much smaller music school in another part of Boston where I would be able to concentrate on learning how to read music and practicing the drums. The first summer that I spent in Boston, I decided to take a philosophy course in the summer school program at Harvard. The professor was an elderly man who was an eloquent speaker and who seemed very passionate in his love for philosophy. After a short time, it was obvious to me that he was a religious man. I could tell by comments and inferences that he made that he *knew*. Listening to him, I could tell that he obviously had had a deep religious experience. I asked to speak with him privately and he agreed. While we were sitting together, I told him about what had happened to me when I was sixteen and that this had been the most extraordinary event in my life. I explained how no one whom I had told about this had been able to understand what I was speaking about. I told him that the conviction that had been so strong in me had begun to fade. I explained how in the time that had elapsed since the event occurred, the living fact of what had revealed itself to me was becoming more and more only a memory. He responded to me by saying that indeed I had experienced a profound revelation and that now I was in the state of what he called "the falling away." He said that I should be patient and hope that it would happen again.

The next two years were uneventful and a time of confusion and discouragement for me. I stayed in Boston for some time, spending much of my time alone practicing the drums and entertaining fantasies of becoming a great musician. Eventually I decided to move back to New York so I could study with a very prominent drum teacher whom I had heard about years earlier. I had hoped that by studying with this man I would be able to develop the kind of confidence that I had never had. This was not to occur. In spite of spending long hours every day practicing and practicing, the self-doubt that had plagued me since my childhood continued to torture me. In addition to the drums, during this early period of my return to New York, for a short time I also studied the vibraphone and then the piano. I auditioned for a few bands through an ad I put in the newspaper and was unsuccessful. What often would happen to me was that I would be overwhelmed with fear and tension when performing my lesson for my teacher and when auditioning or playing with other people. In those moments I felt out of control and at times even felt I could not control my limbs. A growing sense of desperation would come and go, but it was still unthinkable to me at the time that I could fail. Every so often I would recall the splendor of what had revealed itself to me in that brief episode five years earlier and suddenly all that I was doing would be brought into question. When I finally did form a band with some other musicians whom I met through my ad in the newspaper, after only two or three months that too ended in failure and disappointment. I was discouraged and began to seriously doubt if I had what it took to be the kind of musician I wanted to be. At that point I looked very deeply and asked myself this question: "If I were to become a great and renowned jazz drummer and if I were to play the most fantastic drum solo in front of a huge audience and receive a standing ovation – would that make me happy? Would I be satisfied? Would I be content?" The answer came, "No, I would not." For it began to be clear to me that there was something beyond any kind of worldly success that was calling me and that had been calling me. I realized then that only direct knowledge of that alone would satisfy me. I decided to abandon my dream of becoming a great musician, and with confidence in that decision, I went to visit my mother who was at that time living with her second husband on a small island in the Caribbean. I went there with the clear intention to decide what to do with the rest of my life.

SEEKING

2

While on the island I made up my mind to devote
my life to the rediscovery of THAT which had revealed itself to me six years earlier. I had no doubt
that it was only THAT that I wanted, and was absolutely sure of something for the very first time in my
life. A few months prior to this I had begun to take
some classes in martial arts in New York and met a
very inspiring young American teacher. He was at
that time twenty-eight years old, I was twenty-two.
I returned to New York with new found inspiration
and immediately went to see him. He asked me what
it was that I wanted from martial arts training and I
replied, "Self-Realization." He smiled. I soon became
very devoted to this man. I was tremendously inspired by what seemed to me at the time, his tremendous strength, humility and deep spirituality. He was
soft-spoken and confident and very self-assured. He
had, it seemed, read almost every spiritual book ever
written and we would spend hours speaking together
about spiritual matters and the nature of Truth. My
life soon revolved completely around my daily classes
with him. I began to wake up very early in the morning to read spiritual books in the quiet before the
dawn. My teacher had indicated to me that in due

time he would teach me how to meditate, and explained that that also was part of the training. I eagerly awaited that moment. When more than a year had gone by and he still had not yet taught me how to meditate, I decided to pursue meditation on my own. I initially taught myself how to practice Zen meditation from a book. I had been very inspired by reading the book *Autobiography of a Yogi* by Paramahansa Yogananda. His descriptions of Kriya Yoga, a form of Kundalini Yoga meditation, attracted me. Also the writings of Gopi Krishna, describing his fantastic kundalini Awakening after disciplined meditation for fifteen years, fascinated me. The glory and majesty that both these men described in their accounts of their spiritual experiences reminded me strongly of my own Awakening experience.

After seeing an ad in the newspaper, I went to meet an Indian Swami, who was at that time seventy-five years old and was a direct disciple of Paramahansa Yogananda's Guru. He was a master of Kriya Yoga and had mastered the Raja Yoga technique to such a degree that he was able to go into nirvikalpa-samadhi (a deep meditative trance) at will by taking only one inhalation – a very rare achievement. I took a Kriya Yoga initiation from this unusual man and from him learned the art of concentration and meditation. I had never met a human being like this before – someone so obviously "holy." He spoke with a melodious lilt in his voice and possessed an unusual sweetness that expressed a condition of being that I had never seen

before. I was struck by the depth of love and innocence he possessed, but was at the same time puzzled
by the confusion in the people that I saw around him.
This disturbed me and I wondered about it. I took up
the practice of yoga meditation morning and evening,
and when the Swami was in town, went to his small
center every morning to meditate with him. I found
his presence and physical company tremendously
inspiring, and the meditation technique that he had
taught me very powerful. It would often send me into
a state of bliss and profound stillness. My life at that
time revolved around this meditation practice, working and going to my martial arts classes every evening.
After I had been practicing the yoga meditation for
six months, the Swami told me that I was ready for
the second initiation, which was when he would
instruct me into a more advanced practice which
involved subtle breathing methods coupled with
concentration on the chakras. The day after he initi-
ated me, while I was meditating with him and a
small group of people, I had an unusual experience.
It suddenly felt like the bottom of my spine was
plugged into a wall socket, because I felt an enormous
surge of energy rushing from the bottom of my spine
up to the top of my head and all I could see was
blazing white light. The surge of energy was so
powerful that I even thought that my body might
explode. This event lasted a short time, and at the end
of the meditation I could not speak, but could only do
my best to control myself from bursting out laughing.

I was amazed, fascinated and tremendously inspired.

During this period I would go to meet many spiritual teachers that passed through town. I was curious and wanted to know and learn as much as I could. I met and spent time with several swamis, a Hasidic rabbi, a Sufi master, a Zen master and even went to visit Christian faith healers. I wanted to know what was real and what was true. I was always thinking about things my martial arts teacher had said, things my Indian Guru had said, and considered seriously everything that I was learning and experiencing.

After two years as his student, my relationship with my martial arts instructor started to change. With the death of his father he slowly began to lose his self-assurance and inspired disposition. I had been fascinated by the challenge of the physical intensity of the martial arts and attracted to the confidence that its eventual mastery promised me. At this time, instead of encouraging me to do more and more, my teacher began to tell me repeatedly that I should take it easy, rest and not overdo it. Other students noticed the change in him and were also confused by his behavior. I was troubled by this and also gradually became aware of the fact that his knowledge of spiritual matters was more limited than I had originally believed.

I went on a short vacation to Italy to visit a girlfriend, and together we travelled to Switzerland to hear J. Krishnamurti speak in Saanen. At the time I went to see him, I knew absolutely nothing about him or his teaching, except for the fact that he was supposed to be a "living Buddha," and that as he was getting very old, I should not miss the opportunity to see him. Upon entering the large tent in which he was giving a public talk, I was struck by his physical presence and rare beauty. The subject of his talk was the question: does all violence stem from thought? I had absolutely no idea what he was talking about and did not understand most of what he was saying. In spite of this, I made up my mind to stay with every word he said with one-pointed concentration, and I did so for the entire talk. Whenever I noticed my mind wandering, I instantly brought it back to the sound of his voice and to what he was saying. At the end of the talk I still hadn't understood most of what he had said, but was intrigued and interested in this man and his teaching. I went with my girlfriend to take a nap that afternoon and upon waking I felt different. I knew something had changed. At first I wondered if the change was physical, but after looking deeply I realized that this change had nothing to do with my body. I realized that I felt different because I was seeing in a new way. There was a profound sense of objectivity in me that was thrilling. What thrilled me so much was this: for some time I had felt very sure about where I was going and how I was going to get there. Now suddenly I knew that I must not allow myself to take anything for granted – that I should be willing and interested to question absolutely everything. This new perspective excited me tremendously and I felt liberated in the freedom to find out for myself in a way that I had not yet known before.

3

My Indian Guru often said he was "free like a bird and could fly away at any time," which meant that he was not attached to any place; he freely travelled from one city to another and from one country to another. I reflected on this deeply and yearned to be free in that way myself. I loved being around him and serving him gave me great joy as it allowed me to be in his intimate company. The obvious direct knowledge and ongoing experience of the Absolute that he seemed to be immersed in, I yearned for. I grew close to him and would often help to serve him during his stays in New York. I continued to be perplexed and disturbed by the degree of confusion in many of the people close to him and also by his seeming lack of interest in doing anything about it. As a matter of fact, he seemed to perpetually attract confusion, and many of the centers that he started were always doomed to failure because of this.

In 1980 when I was twenty-five, a friend of mine told me that he had been to a Buddhist meditation retreat center where one could meditate through the entire day. He described to me that in these retreats they followed a simple concentration technique and would sit from eight to sixteen hours a day. This intrigued me. A year later, after a painful breakup with a woman I had been deeply in love with, I decided to go to one of these retreats in order to have the experience of immersing myself in meditation all day long. I went to two ten-day retreats that were back-to-back. The retreats were led by two well-known American teachers. These retreats turned out to be an incredibly powerful experience for me. I had never sat in meditation for so many hours at a time, and the depth and power of the concentration that I developed within only a few days seemed extraordinary. This was the first time that I had ever been exposed to Buddhist thought, and I learned for the first time a technique of looking at the mind and body with objectivity. This was fascinating and very liberating. I had two very powerful experiences during those twenty days, both of a very different nature, and I was tremendously inspired by them. A renewed conviction to give myself fully to meditation and to the possibility of Liberation overwhelmed me. I left the retreat with my mind made up that I would abandon the life I had been living in order to give myself utterly and completely to that end.

The next two years were a time of struggle and disillusionment for me. The slow decline in the spirit of my martial arts instructor was difficult for me to accept because he seemed to be unwilling to recognize what was happening to himself or the effect he was having on his students. We experienced a growing frustration with his inability to inspire us and also with his need to remain fully in control of what seemed to be a sinking ship. Even though I talked with him directly about the difficulty we were having and the confusion his behavior was creating, he remained aloof and insisted that nothing was wrong. The fact that I had spent several years with this man and had looked up to him for so long made it difficult for me to let go of the situation, although after much turmoil I finally did. Also with my Indian Guru I had turbulent times. When I was travelling with him on an airplane from Washington, D.C. to Edmonton, Alberta, I shared with him how fascinating it had been for me to do the intensive meditation retreats. I told him the story of how one day after I had been sitting still for a long time, my head started to turn spontaneously in the very same motion that he had taught me as part of the yoga meditation technique. I asked him excitedly what the connection was between this spontaneous occurrence and the deliberate action I was practicing in his technique. He replied in a loud voice, "You are practicing wrong!" and was obviously disturbed by this. A few days later, when I mentioned to him in the gentlest of terms that some of the people he was choosing to represent him were bound to make trouble for him in the future, he expressed displeasure and made it clear that I should leave the matter alone. I did so, but this was the beginning of the end of our relationship. I was in a period of limbo for a while, where I neither had the courage and conviction to leave everything behind me, nor did I have the clarity of intention and confidence to stay where I was. For over a year I lived an odd life, staying in a small room on my own, meditating daily, travelling to different parts of the country to do meditation retreats with different Buddhist teachers and practicing martial arts by myself at the local YMCA. At one of the meditation retreats I attended, I was very impressed and inspired by an English meditation teacher who led the retreat. He was the only one of the Buddhist meditation teachers I had seen who seemed to have had a genuine Awakening. His confidence and sense of humor seemed at the time to express a freedom that none of the others had. I attended several retreats with this man and ultimately decided to go to India to attend a meditation course that he gave every year in Bodhgaya, the site of the Buddha's Awakening.

4

I arrived in India on January 3, 1984 and was intrigued and excited by the strange and unusual new sights, sounds and smells. I felt myself to be on a wild new adventure and it seemed that, temporarily at least, all the burdens of the past had lifted. I made my way slowly to Bodhgaya. There I met many people in a very short period of time, and for the first time in my life felt the freedom to truly be myself. It was pure joy to be able to speak so freely about spiritual matters with people who were interested and also searching themselves.

When I left Bodhgaya I travelled to Puri, a holy
city on the Bay of Bengal. I spent an extraordinary six
weeks there, meditating and feeling a depth of inspiration and confidence in the possibility of Liberation
that I had never known before. After travelling for
some time, I went to Bombay to visit a young Indian
woman whom I had met in Bodhgaya. Her name
was Alka. We fell in love and travelled around India
together, visiting different ashrams and learning
Hatha Yoga. After a year my Indian visa ran out and
I had to leave the country. I travelled to Europe and
then to New York to visit my mother for a short time.
I returned to India at the end of January 1985 and
reunited with Alka in Bodhgaya, where she had
attended the meditation course for the second year
in a row. After several more months in India, it
gradually became obvious to me that I had lost touch
with the profound inspiration I had known the year
before. Feeling strongly that I had lost my way, I
went to England for a few months to meditate with
the English meditation teacher who had inspired me
so much in the recent past. While in England, a friend
told me about a teacher that a friend of his had just
gone to visit in India. This teacher's name was
H.W.L. Poonja. My friend told me that this man was
a disciple of the renowned Indian spiritual Master,
Ramana Maharshi. The minute I heard this teacher's
name I knew that I had to go see him. I returned to
India with my mother, having promised to show her
around this extraordinary country. When we arrived,

we joined Alka and travelled to the Ramana Maharshi ashram in South India, where my friend's friend was staying and where I knew that I could get this teacher's address. As soon as I arrived there I looked for this person, and immediately upon meeting him, he started telling me stories about this unusual teacher. I was profoundly inspired by what I heard and made definite plans to go see him in the near future.

The three of us travelled back to North India, where we all attended the annual meditation course in Bodhgaya. During the course, my mother shared a room with Alka and within a short time Alka became terrified that my mother was going to steal me away from her. I repeatedly told her that this wasn't so and that nothing of the kind was happening. I approached the meditation teacher and asked him for help in this most delicate and difficult situation. He told me that he would talk to Alka and did so shortly afterwards. When I spoke with her the next day, she told me that they had had a great talk. She explained that he had encouraged her to trust her feelings. I was shocked when I heard this because I knew without any doubt that what she had been feeling had nothing to do with the truth. As a result of his advice to her, it became almost impossible for us to have a reasonable conversation. She began to move farther and farther away from me. I became increasingly worried about this and afraid that I would lose her forever. At the end of the course I requested a private meeting with the teacher and asked him why he had told Alka to trust her feelings. I said to him, "Telling a paranoid person to trust their feelings is like throwing gasoline on a fire." I told him that this had been an irresponsible thing to do. When he heard this, he lost his temper and expressed his outrage at my objection to his conduct. I was shocked at his response, and because of the trust I had had in this man, I became profoundly disillusioned. Yet again for the third time, a person whom I had come to trust and revere as Enlightened and who had spoken in detail about living this human life with the highest standards and the purest intention, demonstrated extreme inconsistency and hypocrisy. With my martial arts instructor, my Indian Guru and now my meditation teacher, the same event had occurred. In all three cases, when I made a deliberate attempt to speak honestly and directly with them about inconsistencies in their behavior in relationship to their own teaching, they all responded with anger, outrage or complete disinterest in the very real and important points I was trying to bring to their attention. I was always dumbfounded, perplexed and disillusioned by this kind of response. How was this possible? How could someone who claimed to have given their whole life to the Truth alone and who dared to teach it to others respond in this way?

My relationship with Alka fell apart and I went to Puri by myself to recover from the traumatic effects of the recent events. Also I needed time to think about what to do next. I made up my mind never to involve myself with any kind of spiritual authority ever again. I reflected deeply on the Buddha's parting words, "Be a light unto yourself," and also thought a lot about J. Krishnamurti's insistence that one should never seek for the Truth in any authority outside of oneself. In spite of the shock and disillusionment I was feeling, I had found a new sense of independence and felt that finally I had grown up.

5

After a few weeks in Puri, I made up my mind about what I wanted to do. I knew now that there was no going back. I knew without any doubt that I wanted to go all the way. I knew that I had to be Free and I knew that I could never be satisfied with less than a profound and permanent transformation that had not yet occurred. I concluded that the only way that that could happen was that I needed to make an extraordinary amount of effort towards that end in a way that I had not yet done. I felt that only in this way could I achieve the breakthrough that had so far eluded me. I decided to go to Korea where I would devote myself single-mindedly to the practice of Zen meditation and to a renewed and rigorous study of martial arts. I resolved to not enter into any sexual relationships, without exception, and wanted to live like a monk while I was there. I wanted nothing to interfere with my goal and the attainment of it. I had already acquired information on where to go and how I could achieve this. I resolved that I would not leave for five years, no matter what.

I had written to H.W.L. Poonja asking for permission to visit him and he replied promptly, saying that I was most welcome. I made up my mind that I would go to see him for only three days, and then would continue on to Thailand and from there go to Korea. This was not to be the case.

TRANSCENDENCE

6

I arrived in Lucknow on March 24, 1986. The man
who had given me Poonjaji's address in South India
and who had since become my friend, was in Lucknow
when I arrived and greeted me excitedly. He told me
that Poonjaji was looking forward to meeting me the
following morning. At that time, Poonjaji was living
in his son's house where he had his own room. All I
knew about him was that he was a direct disciple of
Ramana Maharshi and was supposed to be a jnani –
one who had realized the Self. I had read about him
in a book about Ramana Maharshi. The chapter that
was devoted to him described him as a man of intense
devotion to God, profound one-pointedness, and
from what I had read, he seemed to be someone
who was possessed with a personality that was bold
and fearless.

The following morning when we entered his
room, he was sitting on his bed reading some letters
and motioned to us to sit down on the floor in front
of him. My friend touched his feet in the traditional
Indian gesture of respect and then sat down beside
me. Poonjaji was a large man with a beautiful face
and exceptionally striking eyes. After we had ex-
changed greetings, I boldly declared to him that I

had no expectations from this meeting. He replied just as boldly, "That's very good." I immediately felt at ease because it seemed to me at the time that this man wanted absolutely nothing from me. After a few minutes I asked him about the role of effort in spiritual practice. He then said to me very distinctly and very softly, "You don't have to make any effort to be Free." Immediately upon hearing this, something happened. His words penetrated very deeply. I turned and looked out into the courtyard outside his room and inside myself all I saw was a river – in that instant I realized that I had always been Free. I saw clearly that I never could have been other than Free and that any idea or concept of bondage had always been and could only ever be completely illusory. Without thinking, I said to him, "I can now see how just as making effort has become a habit – making no effort could also become a habit." In that instant, he shouted out loudly, "That's it!" I looked up and he was staring at me very intensely. I said to him, "How did you know?" He replied, "When a man sees his own face, he recognizes it!"

Walking with my friend in the street a few minutes after leaving Poonjaji's house, I asked him, "Is it always like this?" I was thrilled and excited and could not quite believe what had just taken place. I wasn't even sure of what had taken place, but I knew without doubt that something extraordinary had just happened.

I spent the next three weeks with this remarkable man. Every day we spent almost the entire day together. I would go to visit him morning and evening and would often stay with him until just before he went to sleep at night. We ate together, went for walks together and often just sat quietly together. During this period, every important question that I had ever had, he answered either directly, with a story or by metaphor. As a result of these talks and this time spent intimately with the man I was soon to call my Master, I gradually discovered that the person who had arrived in Lucknow was no longer the same. I realized that I was dying to everything that I had ever known.

7

I was soon to find that my search had ended forever. But even more incredible than that was that I was about to be catapulted into the most extraordinary adventure that any human being could ever know. The following are excerpts from a letter that I wrote to my mother and brother about the events that transpired over the next five weeks.

> ... When I came to Lucknow to meet Poonjaji five weeks ago, I came here with no expectations and even a fear. I had come to meet another teacher and felt absolutely that I didn't want to

get involved yet again with another teacher, another personality and ultimately more bondage and disappointment. I wanted to be free of all that. So why did I come? I was drawn here and felt I had to come, even though I felt much resistance and fear about what I might be getting myself into yet again. Something 'clicked' on my very first meeting with Poonjaji. We were talking about the need to make 'effort' in practice and Poonjaji said to me that in fact this itself was the problem, that it was in making absolutely no effort at all that freedom could be known. When he told me this, for some reason it penetrated very deeply and I had a sudden understanding that he was right. I 'saw' it and the seeing only lasted two seconds – but it had a deep impact and our relationship began in that moment. I spent almost three weeks with him after that, usually eight hours a day, often talking a great deal and also many times just sitting in silence. Much was gone into and much understood. All the nagging questions that I have had over the last four years about different forms of spiritual experience and the results of different forms of meditation practice were all gone into in depth. All the questions I have had that nobody could help me with, and which had troubled me greatly were all answered. When I told him in detail about the spontaneous awakening that I had when I was sixteen, he told me that at that moment I had experienced all there was to experience, and he said that if I had had a teacher or someone whom I could have talked to about it, a man of knowl-edge – my work would have been over then. Much of what I understood then has returned, and with that and much more I have been able to grasp and understand so, so much. I can hardly believe it all myself. After about a week or so

with this man, finding our talks so, so satisfying,
I unconsciously and consciously surrendered to
him – *realizing that he was only my own Self* and
since then I have been a free being. There is so
much to say and explain! I can't possibly say it
all in a letter. With each passing day he expressed
more and more pleasure at how my understanding was progressing. He many, many times was
praising me and exclaiming things that he saw
were happening which I *never* believed when he
said them. I always felt that he was completely
exaggerating the truth and it made me feel
uncomfortable and caused me to doubt him. But –
I discovered with time that each and everything
that he saw became a living experience for me,
and it only took me time to catch up with him as
ultimately all turned out to be my experience. It is
just that he can see truth directly and due to my
being hypnotized by a lifetime of a very gross
state of awareness – the perception of the *subtle
nature* of the living reality took time for me to
see. I have never ever in my life experienced such
appreciation from another human being. It's all
more than I can grasp! And to be honest I don't
identify with any of it either. It's all part of the
magic as none of what has been understood here
has been understood by Andrew. The ego simply
cannot grasp what is beyond itself. The SELF can
only know the SELF and in this understanding
there is no personality or ego involved. There
cannot be if the understanding is real. Can you
both follow all this? It's really too marvelous and
too wonderful to be believed! When I left
Lucknow two and a half weeks ago he told me
with tears in his eyes that he had never had this
same intimacy with anyone else – and many
people have been Enlightened through contact
with him. Again I just listened passively and

somehow this didn't lodge in my ego – I just
listened and let it go. Nothing, Nothing – I FELT
NOTHING. I know this is hard to believe but it's
true. This *is* true because the core of our relationship doesn't take place between two personalities.
It is only the SELF knowing the SELF. That's why
Andrew felt nothing – for he is *not involved*. What
I am about to tell you both now is something that
I hesitate to tell. I hesitate because it is in fact too
much to be believed. I don't even believe it myself
but I know it's true because it happened.

Poonjaji had told me at one point that he and
I had become one. I said, "You mean Communion" and he told me, "No, Communion is between
two – we are in Union – that means One and not
TWO." Again I didn't believe him or even understand what he was saying. I left Lucknow two and
a half weeks ago and I discovered after saying
good-bye to him that I felt no emotion whatsoever. *None*. This has continued throughout my
trip to Delhi and Bombay and up until my return
to Lucknow five days ago. I understood ultimately that he was right – how can you miss
your own Self? . . . Soon after my arrival in Delhi
the impact of what had taken place in Lucknow
began to make itself known. I spontaneously
began to experience waves of bliss and love that
at times were so strong that I felt my body
wouldn't be able to contain it. But in this Bliss
there was no loss of clarity or understanding.
In fact this only *deepened* much of what I already
understood and in a way I cannot describe in
words – the understanding of what it means to *die
to the known* was lived. It was at times even a little
frightening, as I knew and saw that a part of me
was dying and that I had somewhere stepped out
of this world into the Unknown. I consciously and

unconsciously surrendered – making even a conscious decision to finally let go and give up my life – Andrew's life, for Absolute Freedom – which really means to let go of EVERYTHING. Then the most startling and surprising thing of all happened: People whom I spent time with could feel what had happened to me and were even affected by my presence. I spent five days with a friend – spending hours talking about what had happened in Lucknow and before my eyes – she began to experience the same bliss and understanding that I was! I couldn't believe it, and also somehow it all seemed perfectly natural. . . . The same thing happened with Alka – my God I couldn't believe what was taking place before me! Who would believe it? Who could believe it?

I arrived back in Lucknow five days ago. Since my return much of the bliss has faded and I have returned to an absolutely normal state of consciousness. Nothing but *life as it is*. The only thing is that there is an unbroken sense of continuity and evenness throughout each day. Nothing special. But there is a sense of being always in the present with much contentment and calm. I feel little or no desire for other than what IS and the present moment always feels like enough. . . .

Poonjaji told me two days ago that "our work was over." That we would continue to be friends but our *work* was done. He then said that he wanted me to "accept responsibility for the work." When he said this I just listened passively and accepted what he said without judgement. I have no desire to 'do' any 'work' and I have no aversion to it either. What will be will be and it won't be up to me anymore but to other forces that are Unknown and to which I have surrendered. . . .

After my return to Lucknow I made the following entry in my diary which describes clearly the recognition of my own death and the declaration of my rebirth:

> This I feel must be the end of all that has come before in this record of one man's journey home. It will be the end of that, and then there will be the beginning of the outcome of all that has occurred at the feet of my Master. What will take place from this moment on will no longer be from my own will or desire but will only flow from Him. Andrew's life, in a sense, has now come to an end. His will is my will and his desire my own. I am he and there is total freedom in this. Andrew has no investment or involvement in this in any way. Somewhere Andrew no longer is. He is no longer in control – or desires to be in control. He has surrendered totally and completely to his Master – which is ultimately only his own true SELF. No plans – no personal needs, or painfully unfulfilled desires. He is empty now and is free to be of help – Again – there is no identification with any of this. He has no feeling for or against – there is only surrender and faith. The rest will only be. . . .

Poonjaji told me that I had the same look in my eyes as his Guru Ramana Maharshi did. He said that he had seen these eyes only three times in his life: in his Guru's, in his own and in mine. He repeated that our work together was over. He told me that my understanding of his teaching was total and that he wanted me to go out and help others. He made it clear to me that he now felt free and at peace and no longer felt the burden of carrying on the teaching. He said I could do it now, and for this he was relieved. He told me that he had been waiting for me his whole life and that now he was free.

8

I left for Rishikesh in northern India where I reunited with my friends including Alka, the woman who would eventually become my wife. As soon as I arrived there the teaching spontaneously began to flow out of me and my friends were automatically drawn into my presence. After two days a small group of us rented a room together. The next six weeks proved to be even more extraordinary than the time I had spent with my Guru. It was during this period that I came to accept the reality of what had happened to me. The power, depth and intensity of the clarity that effortlessly was revealing itself to me was so staggering that I again and again thought, "This all must be a dream." We stayed up until the dawn almost every night, and as soon as we opened our eyes in the morning, we would continue this marvelous and ecstatic investigation into and discovery of the Real. We were in a constant state of revelation and I remember one day as we were walking together along the Ganges saying to myself, "This is Nirvana."

Poonjaji wrote me a letter in which he said, "[I want to] leave you ALONE, FREE and INDEPEN-DENT. You have to take up the entire responsibility to help the true seekers with no teaching or any kind of foothold for the mind to abide." I called my mother back to India because as I had felt she was one of my closest friends, I wanted to share this with her. When I went to meet her in New Delhi, I introduced her to my Guru at which time he boldly declared to her that I was *His* Son. He also told her with tears in his eyes, "You don't know how rare this is. Something like this," pointing his finger at me, "only happens once in several hundred years." We spent a few more weeks together in Rishikesh. Upon leaving, the friend who had introduced me to Poonjaji and who had now invited me to England to teach, visited Poonjaji on his way back to Europe. Before he left India my friend wrote me a letter. He told me that in speaking with Poonjaji about me, Poonjaji had said that I would start "a revolution among the young," and that "so far no one has been able to do it."

A month later before I left India, I spent a few days with Poonjaji in New Delhi. We were sitting together on a bench in a park near his daughter's house when he told me that he wanted me to "settle" in America. He explained that he wanted me to go to a beautiful place "where people could come." I said to him, "Master, one of the things that I have admired and respected you for is that you have never created anything. You are asking me to do something that you would never do." He said, "That's right!"

9

I arrived in England at the end of September and began teaching immediately. I started in my friend's living room, and after several weeks moved into a two-story house on a large farm in the country with Alka and a few others who had been with me in India. The word spread fast. Something extraordinary was taking place and many began to hear about it. I lived my days and nights in a state of awe and wonder, always amazed and stunned at the glory and mystery of what was taking place. Surrender was my every breath and the ecstasy of Self-discovery and unimaginable insight was my natural state. The mysteries of the universe, of life and death and all the infinite subtleties of the human predicament and Liberation from it, were constantly revealing themselves to me. A most passionate correspondence began between my Guru and myself. I wrote him ecstatic letters expressing my gratitude and awe at what was taking place around me. I would merely put my pen to paper and my heart would sing songs of love and praise to him who had bestowed upon me the gift of perfect Enlightenment in this birth. He would always respond expressing equally passionate praise and ecstasy at my success and "victory" in this rarest and most dangerous of tasks: to Enlighten others and set them free from the illusion of bondage and separation. My confidence grew and grew and I was amazed to discover that almost no one knew anything about this precious secret that had been revealed to me. Many talked about it, wrote about it and some taught others how to meditate in order to pursue that most elusive and subtle realization. But almost no one, I came to discover again and again, really knew anything about it. Not only that, but soon I found that even those that did know something about this secret from their own experience had stopped far, far short of where I seemed to have come. This amazed me, for where I found myself seemed to have no limit, and this fact at times frightened me because I knew that the implications of this knowledge would threaten many. Several people whom I had known before and whom I had assumed would be interested and excited to share in this realization with me were intimidated and threatened by me. I could not control my exuberance or the ecstatic condition that was the expression of that Source which spoke so powerfully and directly. Those that had any investment in being special found me to be an unbearable presence. I could not and would not control my passion for the Truth.

I spent four months in England teaching six nights a week. What had begun as a small group started to grow in numbers. Many of those who had been deeply affected by my presence and teaching became more and more passionate in their own joy and interest in Self-discovery. I was often amazed to hear words of exquisite beauty and profound wisdom falling from the lips of those who sat around me. I never kept any idea of what should be, in my mind. Often when I would sit in front of the group I would burst out laughing and exclaim out loud to them that I had no idea who they were looking at or what they expected me to say. I chose to avoid safety at all costs and never allowed myself to be predictable. I knew that the source of this knowledge was the unknown and I never allowed my mind or feelings to interfere with its pure and unadulterated expression. My Guru wrote to me, "I hug you and kiss your HEART! And Love my own Self like Narcissus." In another letter he wrote, ". . . I must hand over my robe to you."

10

*D*uring the month of February Poonjaji had been invited by an old disciple of his who was living in New York to come and visit. He did so, and I flew from England and spent three weeks in New York where I stayed with my mother and visited him daily. His disciple knew few people, and when I went to visit in the afternoons the three of us would spend our time quietly together. A few people came to visit him. This time with him was difficult for me for reasons that would only make themselves clear in the future. There was an odd sense of separation between us which made me profoundly uncomfortable. I loved this man with all my heart and he seemed like a god to me – but at the same time it was difficult for us to truly speak freely together. I could not control my desire to share with him all that I was realizing, but found again and again that he seemed unable to hear it, and more often than not preferred to speak mainly about himself and his past.

I went to Amsterdam in early March where I had been invited to teach. Soon many of the people whom I had met in England came to see me and lived together there. They often invited me to visit them, and it was during these visits that I came to understand that those who were united in their love and interest in my teaching, *simply in being together* seemed to be automatically drawn into and immersed in that bliss and love that was impersonal and transcendent. This amazed me. I knew then that the power and implications of what was occurring were far beyond anything I had previously imagined.

My ecstatic correspondence with Poonjaji continued. I wrote to him:

> . . . I feel safe in NOT KNOWING. I feel protected in a sense by my own innocence. I know I am not the doer in spite of the way it seems and in that I am safe. I am only Your Servant and in that service I know only You. In You I am not and if I am not – there is TRUE FREEDOM and LOVE. UNKNOWN LOVE belongs to NO ONE and LOVES only ITSELF. In that LOVE – how could anyone do anything for any other? . . .

He replied:

> . . . How Happy I AM to see every one Loves
> you. Everyone who loves you directly loves me.
> All those who come and Surrender to you will
> instantly win *FREEDOM*. . . .

After three months in Amsterdam I went to Israel where I had been invited to Jerusalem to teach for a month. A group of my students, including my mother, came with me. I returned to Amsterdam at the beginning of August, and after a week left for India where I went to spend three weeks with Poonjaji in Haridwar, a holy city on the Ganges River in northern India. This time with him proved even more difficult than the time I had spent with him in New York six months earlier. He would not allow me to bring up or discuss the explosion that was occurring around me and I found this unbearable. There was so much I was learning and I wanted passionately to share it all with the one who had bestowed the gift of Grace upon me, but it was impossible. One night when we were sitting alone together, I said to him, "Master, it feels unnatural not speaking about what is happening around me." He replied, "Not speaking is speaking." The only time I was able to broach the subject of my teaching was one day while we were waiting for a bus together. I said to him, "Master, it's incredible how perfectly the very essence of your teaching is being expressed through me in my own words." I was surprised when he responded by saying, "No, no it's much more than that." I found that in his company the profound freedom and limitless knowing that had been my natural state since our first meeting was lost. This dumbfounded me. A disciple of his who was there at the time told me later that I had seemed like a caged lion. On the eve of my departure I was in New Delhi with Poonjaji when he asked me to go and buy a particular kind of Indian snack. He explained to me the exact location of the shop he wanted me to purchase it from. When I came back ten minutes later with the snack, he looked at it and found that this one was slightly different than the one that he had wanted. He burst into a rage and began shouting, telling me that I had gone to the wrong shop. I went downstairs with him and he showed me where the correct shop was, just across the street from the one I had been to. There he continued shouting angrily in Hindi to the store owners about how stupid I had been. I had noticed this erratic quality in his personality several times. There was such a stark contrast: on one hand this man possessed an extraordinary sweetness and almost childlike innocence that was so attractive, and on the other hand he could fly into an irrational tirade for no apparent reason. When I arrived at the airport in New Delhi to board the plane back to Holland, the freedom and knowledge that had eluded me for the past three weeks overwhelmed me once again.

11

On my return to Europe I spent a very successful
week teaching in Holland and then went to England
where I stayed for four months. More and more
people were coming to see me, and the power and
effect that my teaching was having on so many only
increased my confidence and inspired me even more.
People came from different places to see me and some
rented houses so they could live together during my
stay there. Several well-known Western Buddhist
meditation teachers came to visit me and I was
shocked to see how little they knew about the mystery that I was sharing with so many. It was becoming
more and more apparent to me the threat that my
absolute stand and unbridled passion and confidence
seemed to pose for many of them. One man who used
to be a Buddhist monk and whose meditation retreats
I had attended, after requesting a private meeting
with me, proceeded to tell me that even though I
didn't realize it, I was "hypnotizing" people. When
I heard this, I did all I could to control myself from
bursting out laughing. He insisted very sincerely that
I should seriously think about this. After listening to
this for an hour, I asked him to simply consider this
possibility: I said to him, "What if people were actually Awakening here and now? Don't you think if
that were actually true, that it would be the most
beautiful thing that could ever happen?" He replied

very slowly, "Yes . . . it would be." Then suddenly he shouted, "That's what I mean – you're doing it right now!"

There were many more events like this. Again and again those who had an investment in knowing something or being somebody seemed unable and unwilling to recognize the power and depth of the extraordinary explosion that was taking place around me. In the Buddhist community many who had practiced meditation very seriously for years were abandoning their practice and sometimes even their lives to be with me. This caused quite a stir and many found the fact of this kind of intensity of passion for Liberation unsettling and disturbing. They seemed incapable of being able to understand what happens to a human being when the fire of Liberation begins to burn in their veins. The words from my Guru, "He is going to start a revolution among the young," came back to me again and again. And I sat and watched this unfolding before me with awe, wonder and tremendous excitement.

12

I had been invited to come to America to teach by one of my students. Poonjaji returned to New York the following year to stay with his disciple again for a few months. I left with three of my students to visit Poonjaji in New York where I stayed for five days.

My students went on to Massachusetts to prepare
for my arrival there and I returned to Europe where
I spent a month teaching in Amsterdam followed
by another month teaching in Rome. Those last two
months in Europe were very powerful and I could
see before my eyes that many of the people that had
been drawn to me were growing ever more strong in
their passion for Liberation and seemed to be pulled
to leave their lives behind them to follow me in this
adventure into the unknown. The excitement was
ever present and I knew no more than anybody
else where it was all leading.

In March 1988 I went with a large group of
my students to live in Amherst, Massachusetts. We
stayed there for six months. On April 13th I wrote
Poonjaji the following letter:

> Beloved Holy Father,
> There is absolutely no doubt that a true revolu-
> tion in consciousness is exploding here in the west
> around your own true son. The speed and power
> of this explosion is impossible for the mind to
> comprehend. Father it is only now that the true
> magnitude of this historic event is beginning to
> dawn on me! Oh Master! TRUTH is such a RARE
> JEWEL in this barren world! Master what has
> happened between us has started a raging fire –
> all of my students are burning with this fire of
> Love and Truth. A revolution has truly begun! I
> am speechless before you – all of this you knew
> from the beginning! Oh Master, who could ever
> believe that such a Holy fire could rage in the
> Hearts of so many? My Father the unknown Love
> is consuming many, many people and all have

only one desire – to stay together and abide as one in this Unknown mystery where all appearances dissolve. . . .

The supreme power, *Your Will*, has consumed your son totally Father. He teaches and preaches only one thing – "ENLIGHTENMENT, ENLIGHTENMENT, ENLIGHTENMENT HERE AND NOW." Nothing else Father nothing else. Only absolute Freedom from the known, Freedom from time and all the creations of a fictitious mind and ego. . . .

During the last two months and increasing in intensity over the last ten days I have been aware of the fact that I am dying more and more. As my name and fame continue to grow I feel more and more distant. The knowledge of who I am and what I am doing becomes less and less clear. I feel with each passing day that I am becoming more transparent and more distant. I feel less and less connected to this world Father – I feel that I am looking at this existence from a place that is far, far away. This detachment, this distance is growing as my fame grows. The more famous the teacher becomes, the smaller Andrew grows. The more Andrew is known, the less Andrew knows. A strange life this is Father! What an unthinkable destiny you have given me! . . .

Poonjaji replied:

. . . You are seated at the SOURCE, from where the sound emerges to become a word. I am very Happy to learn what is going on and most Happy to see who is at the back of all this phenomenon keeping still and unconcerned. You will yet be surprised what is in store. Andrew + ME will witness this Drama in a near future. . . .

On August 18th I wrote to Poonjaji:

... All of THAT which is unfolding around your own true son is without a doubt absolutely KNOWN by Father and son. There is no mistake, no accident and no doubt. This FACT simply IS. My Infinite Father this unbearable Holiness is the most powerful weapon in the universe. It is unstoppable. This FACT is unavoidable. In light of this truth – ALL MUST BE DESTROYED. It has become clear to me that my one and only mission is to destroy absolutely. This LOVE that you have given me is my sword. You have sent me away from You with this one instruction and it is this FACT that has been revealing itself to me again and again and again. This responsibility is unbearable for the mind to even consider, but there is *NO CHOICE*. Having NO CHOICE I must *ACT*.

ALL MUST BE DESTROYED!

At this time, many people are coming each evening for Satsang. About one hundred are here from Europe. Three quarters of the people are giving up everything to follow me. I have not asked them to do so. They are all feeling compelled to follow me. I realize that is my one and only duty to my Master that I must most perfectly NOT RESIST this explosion and simply allow this unthinkable Holy Drama to unfold as it will. I prostrate to YOU my Father again and again and again.

We are moving to Boston at the end of this month and I plan to stay there for about four months. ...

In November I went to India with Alka. After spending a few days with her family in Bombay I flew to Lucknow to spend a week with Poonjaji. I stayed with him at his son's house. I spent all of the time with him and experienced the same uncomfortable sense of separation that had plagued my visits with him since "our work together was over." I couldn't understand it. I loved this man so dearly. I worshipped him. He was the sun that lit up my life. We wrote ecstatic letters of love and devotion to each other, but when we actually spent time together it always seemed like there was little to talk about. I had no doubt that he loved me, but I still could not understand why he did not seem to want to know more about the details and endlessly new discoveries I was making in the midst of the miraculous event that he had proclaimed would occur. I remember him saying something to me, which at the time seemed strange and difficult for me to understand. "I'm only jealous of one man," he said. "Who was that?" I asked. "The Buddha," he replied, "he's the only one who surpassed me."

I returned to Bombay where I attended Alka's sister's wedding. After that we flew to England where I taught for one week and then returned to Boston. On January 8th I wrote him the following letter from Cambridge:

. . . After leaving India on November 18th, Alka and I flew to England where we spent ten days. My students there organized one week of Satsang to be held for seven consecutive evenings. Over two hundred people came, many from different parts of Europe. The photos I have sent you are from this week. We arrived back in Boston at the end of November. The last month has been very busy with Satsang five nights a week and a lot of work being done on the book that I told you about when I was with you in Lucknow. . . .

The Mystery of *YOUR GRACE* Father, is really what this book will be about. Through our correspondence it shows in a very rare way the Unbearable LOVE between Father and son. The meaning of SURRENDER and of LOVE for the MASTER. . . . It is fantastic Father because it was you who told me that I would write a book – You told me this after you had a dream about it over one and a half years ago!

What is happening around me, my Father, through YOUR GRACE – is too fantastic and too beautiful for words. A real SANGHA is growing around me and many of my students are catching my FIRE. There are now twenty houses here in Cambridge where my students are living to-gether. Many have come from Europe and are staying for long periods. This decision to live together and come together to be near me has happened quite spontaneously and naturally. I have not told anyone to do so, but this is their wish. As this has been happening steadily by itself over the last year and a half, a real Sangha is being born. The teaching is ENLIGHTENMENT and the teacher speaks of nothing else. The living understanding of this living truth is being lived by many of my students, and it is only through YOUR GRACE that this is happening.

As each day passes Father I feel my strength and confidence growing stronger and stronger. You told me how truly rare this event is, but it has taken two years for me to understand what you were saying. I could not believe you as it simply seemed *too much to believe*. But now Father, I not only believe but I *KNOW* it's true. And this fact is unbearable and terrifying. But I am not terrified Father. Simply I know, and in this I am at Rest. That which cannot be borne is borne and there is no conflict and no fear. It is all only your Love and GRACE and I simply am not interfering with what feels preplanned and perfect. Oh my Father with each day my recognition of the mission you have given me deepens and with it I feel more and more fire and zeal which is my fuel. The desire that "this living truth must be known" burns within me Father and yet I know fully well that this is not my desire at all but your own. Because the real mystery of it all is that as my fire increases and confidence grows, my own sense of Freedom and detachment also increases. . . .

His reply was:

Very dearly dear Son,

Received your loving letter each word entered my bones and shakes up my body So Happy I always feel whenever I receive news about you and hear from people who come to see me. Some of them have heard of you, even as far as far east and even entire Europe and Latin America. They will go to Cambridge to see you. . . .

What is going on around you is a miracle. You are a gifted person. All my 75 years I could get a

serious, sincere, dedicated, obedient disciple who
moved so close to my Heart Soul and body. When
ever I move I feel I speak through your mouth
and live in your body.

    My Love to you. All my children live happy
and peaceful Life.

In the spring of 1989 I put together with some
of my students a book describing my initial meeting
with my Guru, the explosion that occurred and all
that had happened up until that time. The book was
comprised of excerpts from a diary that I kept during
my meeting with him and also included much of our
correspondence over the ensuing three-year period.
The book was called *My Master is My Self*. Little did I
know then the effect this book was to have. It would
eventually catapult Poonjaji from relative obscurity
into being well on his way to becoming a legend in
his own time.

13

*I*n the early summer of 1989, I moved to Marin
County across the bay from San Francisco with all
of my students, now officially being called "the
Sangha."

Since I began teaching in India in 1986, something has been coming out of me that I have no power

over. It is me and it has possessed me. After my initial meeting with my Guru while sitting alone in a hotel room in New Delhi, I became aware of the fact that there was a "presence" in the room with me. In fact this presence, it seemed, had been following me ever since I had left my Guru a few days earlier. It was inside me and it was outside me. It was haunting me and it was loving me. It terrified me and I was also thrilled and intoxicated with joy because I knew without any doubt that it was the essence of Love itself and none other than my own true Self. I was frightened at the time because I knew and I could see that "it" was consuming "me." The thrill of this knowledge and the unparalleled awe and sense of wonder that came from this knowledge is indescribable. The following morning, instantly upon waking I sat up in my bed, and without thinking I said to myself, "I surrender my life to YOU – do with me what YOU will." When I said this, I meant it. From that moment on, my life was no longer my own. I gave it up. I surrendered. It was all over. Since then, there has been a passion and an intensity that comes out of me when I am teaching and when I am speaking about the Truth that I cannot control and that literally overwhelms me. This passion that comes from nowhere and burns so deeply in my veins *is* the Truth itself. It is this passion that has from the very beginning forced me to tell the truth and to never deceive anyone else about the reality of their own condition. It is this passion that has caused many to feel threatened. The intensity of my call has always demanded everything that a person is able to give – one's whole heart and all of one's soul to the Source itself, from which arises nothing but perfect freedom, true knowledge and the exquisite happiness of knowing that one has come home forever. Truly, there is no other way if one wants to be FREE. It has always been this way and it will always be this way. To receive everything one must give everything. It could not be different. This message has been pouring out of me since the day the Source began expressing itself, and because of this the extraordinary explosion or "revolution" that my Guru predicted would take place has been and is occurring. This is none other than the force of evolution manifesting itself, and I am but a mere pawn in this drama of creation.

From the instant that I first left my Guru many of those whom I came into contact with easily and often instantly began to have profound realizations, insights into their true nature and powerful feelings of love, joy and bliss. This has continued since that time. At first this startled and amazed me and was a source of profound wonder and joy. In the beginning I thought that those initial breakthrough experiences would set a person Free forever, as had happened in my case with my own Teacher. I thought that the penetrating insight into the nature of all things and the overwhelming experience of love, joy and bliss that ensued would, as it did in my case, reveal the

Absolute Truth to such a degree that one would never be able to return back to an ignorant and unenlightened condition. I found that this was not the case. Over the first few years of my teaching, I observed many people soar to unimaginable heights of ecstatic release and profound understanding, and then fall back again into a condition of confusion and unenlightenment. Over time and much scrutiny into this matter, I understood that different individuals had different capacities for Awakening, and any limitation an individual imposed on the depth and degree of their Awakening was ultimately due to pride and pride alone. I came to understand that the initial Enlightenment experience served mainly to reveal the Absolute to a person, and in that realization they were glimpsing their own potential for final Liberation. My Teacher always said someone was "Enlightened" after this initial glimpse into their true nature. I soon realized this wasn't true. If a person was "Enlightened," to me that meant that they had to be able to manifest and express that Enlightenment consistently in their behavior. I had observed so many people who had experienced profound awakenings and yet still would be unable to manifest and express that realization in their outer lives. It seemed that in spite of "Enlightenment," much neurotic and conditioned behavior usually remained. And not only that, I observed also that in spite of temporarily having seen through the nature of mind and thought, many still would be unable to see beyond the subtle concepts and thought formations that were their own mind. What did all this mean? It meant that Enlightenment was only the beginning. It meant that the realization of one's ultimate potential was the beginning of the path. It meant that indeed the beginning of the path was the end of all seeking, but not necessarily the end of realization.

The intensity of the call that has been echoed in my words and in my entire being throughout my teaching career has inspired many to give up everything in order to live a life totally dedicated to the pursuit, discovery, investigation of and abidance in the Enlightened condition. For the first two years of my teaching, I simply observed as many were drawn to follow me. I neither encouraged them nor discouraged them. After three years, I could no longer avoid the fact that what prevented most people from an undivided condition of permanent meditation and Self-discovery was the reluctance to give up everything for it. I observed how most "seekers" were not genuinely serious. It seemed most only wanted to add "Enlightenment" or spiritual experiences to their already confused lives. I observed again and again that "Enlightenment" is not a thing that can be added to another thing, but only an ultimate condition or absolute fact that must be surrendered to. It became clear that the degree to which a person was able to surrender to that absolute fact was the degree to which they would know that fact as their own true

Self or true nature. It was because of this that I began to emphasize the necessity and importance of renunciation for this lofty end. Again and again during my evening teachings, I would be shocked to hear the degree of passion with which I was speaking about this.

The following are excerpts from a letter that a close student of mine wrote to Poonjaji in August 1989:

> . . . It is an incredible and profound Mystery that any sincere and earnest seeker who has come to Andrew with pure intention has found the end of their search in Him. But this, it now appears, is only precipitating a greater explosion. Andrew is burning with a Holy Fire that is unquenchable. His demand is the call of the Source for the heart's complete surrender – to *live* this realization perfectly in this very birth. Nowhere in this world is such an absolute demand being made.
>
> Recently Andrew has become much more directly involved in the community that has formed around him in a way that he has never done before. There are now 30 houses full of his students living in this area of California. Andrew is fearlessly creating form out of what has up until this time remained quite formless. He is forging and shaping tirelessly a noble community that is vibrating with renunciation and Love. How incredible it is that the community that is spontaneously forming around Andrew in the midst of this modern, materialistic society so closely resembles the followings of the great Masters of ancient times.
>
> Many have fallen aside in the face of such an Absolute demand, unwilling to face their own

death in Truth. In such a demand all is revealed
in a human being sooner or later. . . . Samsara and
Nirvana are being constantly revealed in greater
intensity. It is the power and insistence of this
demand which knows no compromise which is
forcing everyone to be entirely and perfectly
responsible to their own heart. . . .

Poonjaji replied:

. . . I am very happy to read again and again
what you have described in your letter. What
Andrew is Teaching, Such Teaching is no where
heard else where in the world. There may be
Preachers of Traditions and never a Teacher of
TRUTH. Who and How any one dare teach or talk
about Truth unless one had a rare Luck to have
been confronted the MAJESTIC MAGIC of the
UNKNOWN *UNCONCEIVABLE* All pervasive
Prajna, That alone Can Speak itself to itself for
itself. I Send my Blessings to you and all of my
children. . . .

The community of students that had gathered
around me by this time had become an entity. The
degree of intensity in which the Truth was being lived
and constantly revealed in that entity was having an
incredible impact on the individuals involved. What
I had only had intimations of three years earlier in
Europe was now becoming more and more clear to
me. There was an extraordinary power that was able
to express itself when a group of individuals came
together in the name of Truth and Liberation. The
intimacy and trust that was being experienced was
so exquisite that time and time again I would observe

myself and many of those around me become overwhelmed with the knowledge that this kind of gathering in its intimacy expressed. It made possible a
knowing of that which is sacred simultaneously in the
hearts of all in a way that is indescribable. The knowing of oneness, which is the direct experience and
knowledge of the non-dual that was being constantly
known, drew us all again and again into a state of
Grace and profound revelation. This extraordinary
and unusual alchemy that was occurring in, with
and through my students as individuals and as
a whole is the force of evolution. I began to understand that true evolution could play itself out in this
most unusual circumstance where so many had come
together for only one end – to be completely Free.
My constant insistence that the Truth be lived was
having a profound impact. It was creating a situation
where individuals could no longer avoid inconsistencies and hypocrisy in their own being. In light of this,
many rose to my call for evolution, and in this, karmic
chains were being broken and I was observing extraordinary transformation and true emancipation
being realized and lived. My emphasis that all individuals take responsibility for their entire karmic
predicament created a situation where the stakes
were always high and the Truth was the only fact
that never changed. Some found this blazing light
unbearable because in its reflection nothing could be
hidden and nothing could be avoided. The Truth *was*
being known and in that light all would eventually

be exposed. Those who were unwilling and unable to step fully out of the darkness of their own mind and into that light left, because they found the demand for total integrity and absolute responsibility too much. Since that time I have continued to learn and understand that not all individuals possess the same desire and capacity for Liberation. It is indeed rare that an individual is capable, willing and interested in going all the way.

In California I observed that people who were coming to see me found the unusual sacrifice that many of my students were making suspect. Those who were teachers and "experts" in the field of spiritual matters were, to my surprise, the most alienated by the intensity with which the Truth was being lived around me. They found the honesty, ecstasy and passion in my students and the life that we were living threatening and difficult to comprehend. Many presumed it was wrong only because they could not understand it. Something like this cannot easily be understood when only casually observed from the outside. When some, being unable to rise to the standards that were being asked then left, public opinion found "proof" that something indeed must be very wrong. In actuality, the revolutionary nature of the explosion that we were all living was working to an extraordinary degree. This was proved by the very fact that those who were unwilling or unable to meet the challenge to evolve could not find anywhere to hide. This continues to be the case. When the light of Truth is blazing brightly nothing can be obscured. This has been and always will be the revealing power of the Truth itself when it is shining with unhindered purity. Not all are equally able to rise to the highest. This is an evolutionary fact and has historically been called the law of karma. Karma cannot be avoided and the light itself can only serve to reveal the actuality of any individual's karmic circumstance. The sincere interest in an individual to face the entirety of their karma in the light of the Absolute Truth and their ability to bring it all to an end, will be the degree to which they will be able to Awaken. Not all people are the same and different people have differing capacities for this rare evolutionary leap.

14

*E*ver since I was eleven years old and my mother left to live in Italy, we had been close friends. When we were together, we would spend long hours speaking about life, the mind and the struggle to become a human being. When I was young I did most of the listening. It was her interest in psychotherapy that had brought me to psychoanalysis at such a young age. Because of my early intense exposure to looking at my own mind and feelings coupled with a natural sensitivity, I was able from quite a young age to speak about emotional and psychological matters in a way that was unusual for such a young person. Our friendship continued to grow as I got older. A fundamental shift took place though when I was twenty-two years old and consciously turned my life and full attention to spiritual evolution. I brought my mother to meet all of my teachers soon after I met them. When I took up martial arts, she eventually began to learn Tai Chi. When I began to seriously practice Kriya Yoga meditation, I brought her to meet my Indian Guru and she also took the initiation and shortly thereafter stopped smoking. When I decided to attend a Buddhist meditation retreat, she decided to come with me. I had even taken magic mushrooms with her in order to give her a taste of the psychedelic experience. A very sensitive and intelligent woman, she had become fascinated with psychoanalysis and its promise during the late 1940s when it was a new and radical approach to looking at life and the mind. She never had the kind of deep spiritual revelation that I had had. Also in spite of an energetic and enthusiastic personality, she remained troubled by her history, haunted by her failure to become a successful writer and cynical about any possibility of true love and profound intimacy. From the time I was twenty-two, when I began to put my full attention on the spiritual and away from the world, I increasingly began to feel a tension in our relationship. Even though she expressed serious interest in these matters and would even devote time and effort to the practice of meditation, Tai Chi, etc., there always seemed to be an unbridgeable gap between my heartfelt yearning to reunite with my true Self and my mother's mere exploration of a new terrain. As time went on, I felt this gap widening because it became increasingly more difficult for me to speak honestly and passionately to her about spiritual insight and intuitive knowing. She always found it difficult to step beyond the bounds of her intellectual knowledge and tended to reduce everything to the psychological. How to bridge the gap between one who has KNOWN and one who has NEVER known? She was unaware of this gap. In spite of this, I loved her deeply and considered her a dear friend. It was because of this that I excitedly called her back to India to be with me immediately after my explosive meeting with Poonjaji. From the very beginning, she was more disturbed and uncomfortable about the fact that she had "lost" her son than she was in the extraordinary and most rare transformation that had obviously taken place in the soul of the one she had brought into the world.

From the beginning of my teaching I asked her clearly and directly if she wanted me to help her and she said that she did. In spite of this, she was never able to deeply recognize what had happened to me and was never able to truly perceive the extraordinary glory and majesty of the Grace and knowledge that we were in the midst of. It has been said that the family of the one who has Awakened is unable to recognize their transformation, nor perceive its significance. This also has been my experience. My mother had tremendous resistance accepting me as a teacher and insisted on relating to me only as her son. This made it very difficult for me to help her to see beyond her own mind. Even though she consciously chose to become my student, she found the total immersion into the investigation and discovery of Enlightenment too much to bear. The call for evolution that many of my students were rising to, she began to see as fanatical demand for conformity and submission. She could not understand the intensity of the love that my students had for me and felt threatened by their passion and one-pointedness in pursuit of the Real. The depth of spiritual Awakening that was occurring all around her, she began to see as delusion, fear and neurotic need. In the midst of our move to California she went to see the nihilistic anti-teacher teacher U.G. Krishnamurti. I have not seen her since. Painfully she turned against me and even began to publicly denounce me. She felt that I had gone mad and had freed myself from my childhood inferiority by becoming a charismatic leader who held out the promise of heaven and happiness to weak-minded people who would submit to my need to control others. Feeling that I lived in a deluded world of my own making, surrounded only by people who would agree with my every wish and whim and who lived only for my approval and in fear of my rejection, she began to tell others that I was on my way to becoming a Jim Jones. This was painful for me to hear, for in spite of the fact that she had had a tremendous amount of difficulty in letting go of the image of her son and being able to see me for who I had become, she still had had many deep realizations with me and had even, if only temporarily, seen beyond her own mind. Now she had become my enemy and this was one of the most painful events of my entire life. Little did I know that my mother's betrayal and inability to recognize the depth and the purity of what was occurring around me would be the beginning of a nightmare that had only begun to unfold.

15

*I*n December of 1989, I went to England to teach for two weeks. A small group of Poonjaji's intimate devotees came to visit me there. I observed that they seemed to find the seriousness of my call and the passion and renunciation in my students threatening in some way. This surprised me.

From England I went with my wife Alka to visit her family in Bombay, and from Bombay I flew to Lucknow to visit Poonjaji. I stayed with him at his family's house and Alka joined me there for the last three days. I experienced the same odd sense of separation between us and also continued to find it difficult to communicate with him directly about my teaching. For the majority of the time we spent together, he devoted most of his attention to two other students who had come to see him. I still wanted to share so much of what I was endlessly discovering, but this rarely occurred. On two occasions during this visit, out of the blue he praised me quite highly. On the first occasion I was sitting with him in his family's small living room. While he was talking with an Indian man who had come to see him, he compared me with the greatest Indian Rishis (sages) of the past. Also one day when I was sitting in front of him in his room with my wife seated next to me, he slowly began to read to us out loud from a small notebook that he always keeps with him. One after the other he read a list of the names of all of the Buddhas that had come into this world. When he got to the end of the list he read out my name and then looked at me and smiled.

After my return to California, I received the following letter from Poonjaji:

> . . . I am Happy you have returned HOME Safe. My mind hesitated a bit to use this most common phrase return home or let us call it from HOME to HOME or still better in your case is Always at *HOME*. Anyway we live in the world and we should do as others seem to do externally. I was very very deeply Happy to find you more loving, more obedient, most meek and humble, your Surrender stood as strong and Perfect and dedicated as 5 years ago. You were the Man I looked for all my Life. I am Happy now. You can kindle the Light into the Hearts of ignorants of the

universe. I am Happy you have found a sweet
intelligent wife and team of very serious students.
Now the SUN will Rise from the WEST and
Enlighten the universe. . . .

After my return from India, I wrote Poonjaji a
letter describing the natural evolution that was taking
place in the Sangha. I informed him about details of
the many changes in its form that were constantly
occurring. I told him how my most serious students,
who had abandoned the world to live in my community, were now meeting in order to help each other
with any difficulties that arose and also to explore
and inquire together into the vast subject of what
Enlightenment truly is. I explained how I wanted as
many of my students as possible to accept more and
more of the responsibility for this precious teaching.
I wanted to create a situation where each and every
individual would be encouraged to rise to the highest
understanding that they were capable of. I wanted
any possibility of stagnation or limitation obliterated
so that all would have to stand alone in the unknown.
I wanted each individual to be fully responsible for
themselves and what they had realized. This began to
unfold. I spontaneously responded to the needs that
the situation presented and was continuously amazed
to learn how delicate is the human condition and how
fearful most human beings are of truly transcending
any possibility of limitation. Again and again I was
seeing how all human beings are different and have
different capacities for Awakening. Unexpectedly an

insecure individual would transcend deeply held beliefs and suddenly be able to manifest profound freedom and understanding, while some of those who had seemed most confident would crumble in the face of the opportunity to evolve. What a mystery this was! I realized that the burden of karma could be avoided by no one. The fact of Enlightenment seemed to serve as a mirror simultaneously revealing the endless depth of one's true nature and the limitations of the mind and ego. There was, I continued to discover, an unknown factor in each individual that was thoroughly unpredictable. Even though I knew without any doubt that anything was possible at any moment, and that any individual only had to choose to be completely free if they truly wanted to be free of time and thought – *when* anyone would suddenly be able to leap further into the depths of surrender and perfect Liberation was always unknown and mysterious.

I wrote to Poonjaji:

> . . . The fire of renunciation is burning within my students and it is this fire that I am constantly fanning. Renunciation is this life and this life is renunciation. . . .
> My reputation of being a "fierce" and "controversial" teacher is spreading far and wide. . . .

A natural division began to occur between those who were most serious and those who were less serious. A lay Sangha grew of those students who preferred to remain in the world and live a life less rigorous in its demands while still participating in my teaching and community.

Poonjaji wrote:

> . . . I have received your letter dated Jan. 26, 90.
> I am very glad to read it again and again. The
> work allotted to us is being carried out beautifully
> to spread the Love everywhere among all Beings.
> I am very satisfied with my Son and how he is
> able to handle the responsibilities to give Love
> and Peace to the People Living in this universe.
> My dream in finding you has become a reality
> even before I reject the physical sheath, otherwise
> I had carried it along with me to be postponed to
> next incarnation. The 20th Century is lucky to
> have seen the Perfect Buddha reborn to live with
> them to Free them from the miserable samsara
> sagar and not to return to endless cycle of Births
> and Deaths for ever. . . .

In response to a letter and telegram I sent him he replied: "I want to see you on the TOP of the world before I leave my physical sheath."

I wrote to Poonjaji in April 1990 describing events of a recent teaching trip to Colorado:

> . . . Many people expressed excitement and
> *interest* in what I teach – Enlightenment and only
> Enlightenment. In many other places I have been
> people who come seem only interested in bliss,
> but very few who I meet are truly interested in
> the Teaching – Renunciation and Perfect Death

in this life. Especially here in California, because I have so many followers who are so devoted to my Teaching, people who come to see me are suspicious of my Sangha. I think it is the fact that my formal students have been inspired to give up so much to live this life that worldly seekers find this very threatening. . . . I have been feeling for the last few months that there are very few *truly* serious seekers in this world. Very few who are ready to meet my fire with their own passion, very few who are willing and interested in looking into what it truly means to live a life with no future. . . .

The love, joy and emptiness that I see shining in the eyes of my students fills me with wonder and infinite gratitude to You, who have set me forth on this journey. I feel so inspired and I am constantly learning and realizing so much. . . . I feel the work has only just begun and I know that there is much, much more to do. I know there is nothing in my way. Sometimes I am terrified when I realize how alone I am, but this only lasts a few moments and I am overcome with passion and love and the thrill of destiny. For I realize again and again that that which I would never dare to imagine is true. . . .

I am very excited to tell you that I have decided to take all of my students with me to India next winter, where I plan to spend one month in Bodhgaya teaching. Also, it would be my deepest honor to bring my students to meet my Holy Father either before or after. They are all very excited at the idea of my teaching in Bodhgaya and of having the opportunity to meet you and receive your blessing. . . .

I included a letter I had received recently from someone who had been coming to see me for a short time:

Dear Andrew,

I am writing this letter to express my heartfelt gratitude for your recent visit. . . . I have been trying to put you in context – a bit of Krishnamurti, Da Love Ananda, Gurdjieff, Maha Ati, Advaita-Vedanta – so that I could file you neatly into some conceptual corner that I could conveniently reference. Like the best of the above teaching, you defy context, you destroy concept. I have also been looking for errors, for you to fail, so that I wouldn't have to take you seriously. Like the best of teachers, you simply reflected this neurosis back to me.

I don't like to file in with the love and light testimonials, but yes I've had extraordinary dreams and experiences since your visit – in fact I have been living a spiritual metaphor for the past two weeks. These I freely acknowledge and thank you for. The most important event, however, has been the profound incorporation of the immediacy of the awakened state. This "knowledge" is priceless, a gem I have inherited from you.

Most paths climb to a summit, a holy jumping off place, where the last step is to just do it. The jump kills ego, and one finds oneself back where one started – so why start? Your "path" is so steep it is indeed a cliff. In your path the first step takes ego immediately *down*, there is no ascent, there is no path.

I have looked into my motivation for this letter, and it is not to display my level of understanding (or more likely my lack of it), nor to gain some measure of recognition or confirmation. It is to simply say thank you. Thank you for your infinite patience, your fearlessness, your wrath and your humor. Thank you for sharing your heart.

Poonjaji responded:

> . . . Good Luck and good wishes to my dear Son. Keep the Banner of freedom aloft and go around the world to free the suffering race from miserable Life. I am glad to hear from people who visit me about the help you have rendered to them in England and U.S.A. . . .

Over the past two years some people who had come to see me visited Poonjaji and more recently, as a result of reading my book, more began to be curious about him and travelled to India to meet him.

DISILLUSIONMENT

16

*A*nyone who approaches a real teacher of Enlightenment must be ready to question anything and everything. If they are truly sincere about their quest for Perfect Freedom, they must be willing to look deeply. The idea of profound Freedom or "Enlightenment" sounds romantic and thrilling to many seekers, but I have found that few actually have the integrity of interest that is necessary to pursue any and every potential obstruction to that Freedom. I have found that the more invested someone is in who they think they are, the more difficult it will be for them to see clearly. Many "spiritual" people are fiercely identified with ideas of themselves as being "good," "compassionate" or "saintly." Even though they may readily admit neurotic confusion or difficulty, I have found that few who claim that they want to be "Enlightened" are willing to part with *every* idea of who they think they are – "spiritual" or "worldly," pleasing or distasteful, worthy or unworthy. One must be willing to at least LOOK and SEE what's there. So many are so invested in ideas and false images about themselves. I have found it surprising how many "spiritual" people are especially terrified of looking too closely for fear of truly seeing beyond their ideas.

To live with no reference point whatsoever, to see with no reference point whatsoever is the Enlightened condition that is the goal of all sincere seeking. I have never been able to tell anyone that this is not so. This simple truth applies to everyone. Anyone who truly wants to be Free must be willing to question everything. Ever since I began teaching I have always been honest and forthright about this.

During the late spring and early summer of 1990, some people who had come to see me for several months went to visit Poonjaji in India. When they returned, I was told they spoke with extreme disrespect and even contempt about myself and my students. This shocked and surprised me. In my company, these individuals had all behaved only respectfully and with deep appreciation. With few exceptions, I did not see these people again. While they had been with me, I tried to help them. I clearly pointed out false ideas that they had about themselves that were obscuring their own Perfect Freedom. I was startled to hear that apparently Poonjaji had contradicted things I had said to them. Confused, I asked one of my students who knew Poonjaji well to write to him and ask him about the disrespectful conduct. In response, he wrote:

> . . . I am in ecstasy to read what you have mentioned about my Son and all what I continue to hear from all quarters of the world and I am most Lucky Father. I send my Blessings to HIM

and to all of you who stay near him and look after his comforts to arrange the Satsangs of the Dharma. . . . You need not get upset. Most of the People will like to remain in Ignorance. Only a few in the world [will] receive the Teaching and get FREE. There were people who were against Rama, Krishna, Buddha and Jesus. NO ONE can touch my Son. . . . Go ahead with your Dharma and do not Look Behind at the Barking Dogs. All the world and the gods will unitedly do the utmost to Bring back a person from the Dharma to hinder His way to Enlightenment. . . . I am happy He (Andrew) comes to Bodhgaya in Jan. 91. . . .

A few months after my arrival in California, a man came to see me who had heard about me from his friends. He was a psychotherapist (like many in California) who had a background of spiritual practice with an Indian Guru. On the second night that he came to see me he had a powerful experience. His face completely changed. He sat in front of me immersed in bliss, smiling from ear to ear, and expressed deep gratitude. Night after night he would sit in front of me smiling, with his eyes glazed, occasionally making proclamations of devotion and profound appreciation. However I soon began to notice that this man had no interest in any kind of investigation into the nature of the Real. He seemed only to want to sit before me in ecstasy. I thought to myself, how could this man, a psychotherapist, be so disinterested in this extraordinary investigation that is endless and ever new? He would listen with interest as I probed deeply with others who were taking risks and looking together with me beyond the known. Whenever I attempted to draw him into this exploration, it was always impossible to get past first base because he was afraid of real intimacy, true honesty and the sincere reckoning that any human being must undergo if they want to be truly Free. The fact that this man was a therapist, and yet was unwilling to face himself, I found difficult to accept. Again and again I noticed that those who were most strongly invested in ideas about who *they* were found my insistence on integrity in the pursuit of Truth unacceptable. The whole structure of who they thought they were and wanted to remain was absolutely threatened by the intensity of my honesty and passion in and for the Truth itself. It is this that I have not been able to compromise for *anyone*. How can *anyone* claim that they want to be Free and be unwilling to face themselves? I have always insisted that anyone who claims they want to be Free, be willing at least to look and to question – without this willingness how can any possibility of true understanding unfold? After a few months, I told the therapist that I could not accept his absolute unwillingness to face himself.

Over the last almost six years I have met so many people like this. Psychotherapists, meditation teachers, false gurus, workshop leaders – "helping professionals" all so invested in and identified with what they think they are doing. Surprisingly I have found so many unwilling and unable to be simple and truly honest. It has been and continues to be a revelation to me how so few are able to be sincere when faced with the possibility of going all the way home. Instead of considering that most rare possibility with true maturity and a sincere reckoning of absolutely everything, most approach the possibility of Enlightenment seeking for only affirmation and confirmation of who they already are. A deeply honest reckoning will always bring the sincere individual to the obvious conclusion that THIS IS IT. Most are unwilling to take the risk of truly dying to the known, which means letting go of any and every idea of who they think they are, and in doing so facing their maker here and now. What is one who is unwilling to compromise the Truth for anyone to do?

The therapist who had sat before me immersed in bliss insisted he was sincere. He could not understand what was wrong. He could not understand why his "love" was not enough. Why did I insist he was not serious? I told him, "You're afraid of being nobody."

In the initial time I had spent with Poonjaji, we were alone most of the time. I had been at first shocked and then impressed by his fierce criticisms of false teachers and insincere seekers. I would listen aghast as he would, with absolute confidence, speak about the corruption of renowned gurus and would boldly proclaim how most of humanity was only like "pigs and dogs" in their inability and unwillingness to recognize or treasure the rare preciousness and perfect purity of the Self.

When the therapist who was afraid of being nobody came back from a visit to Poonjaji with an Indian name, and very proud of it, I was amazed. I was amazed because he was full of an arrogant confidence that surprised me. He approached a student of mine whom he had brought to me and asked her to please relieve him of the karma of having introduced her to me! This was only the beginning of a long line of incidents that slowly began to reveal that my Master and myself were not seeing through the same eyes. Many people who were unable to meet my demand for simple integrity, found in my Master "unconditional love" and "acceptance." It began to appear that my Guru was willing to compromise where I could not.

17

*I*n spite of the odd sense of separation that occurred when I was in the presence of my Master, and in spite of aspects of his personality and conduct that expressed contradiction, I still had no doubt that the fairy tale was still a fairy tale and that on the deepest level we were deeply in love and perfectly at one. I still believed everything he had told me about how he felt about me and never questioned the fact that he was my Father and that I was his Son. Slowly more and more people were travelling to India to visit him. I wrote to him at the beginning of July:

> ... Master I have been learning so much and I am constantly amazed at the unimaginable power of ENLIGHTENMENT. This vision is too much for an ordinary man to bear. In order to keep this jewel intact and alive it is necessary to give up everything for it – simply to *BE FREE*. Master the power of this clarity that you have bestowed upon me has *No End*. It is *Limitless*. This clarity can penetrate any thought and look directly into the very depths of this human existence. Often what I see is hard to bear as I realize again and again how few people in this world want to be truly Free. This fire burning inside me wants only to consume those pure hearts that come to me and to destroy the ignorance in those who insist on the reality of their own minds. Master this passion burning inside me threatens many people. As you may know there are some people that have come to visit you who insist on making a distinction between Father and Son. How could the Father be different from the Son? Master so few in this world want to truly know this precious truth of Perfect Enlightenment!

Also in this letter, I asked Poonjaji if some recent news I had heard was true. I had been told that someone who had been my student and who had visited Poonjaji in India had been given an Indian name, proclaimed to be a "satguru" and asked to teach by him. I had heard by this time several similar stories about others over the past three years that had all turned out to be false rumors. This had always confused me because I knew that to dare to teach another about the precious jewel of Enlightenment was indeed the highest calling for a human being, and to do so that human being had to be perfect. Always when I had heard these stories it had caused me to temporarily doubt my Master because I knew directly or indirectly several of the individuals involved, and knew without any doubt that they were far from the immaculate condition that is the holy ground from which the Self can express itself perfectly and without even a trace of interference. Even one speck of dust left on the mirror that reflects the Self will hinder and influence to some degree the perfect reflection of the Source of our being. The inherent danger of one who dares to bring others to Enlightenment, without having been utterly and absolutely consumed themselves, is that any traces of ignorance that may remain due to undissolved pride and desire will mar and influence the reflection of the Self and will defile the transmission of perfection. Most who dare to take on the role of Master – even though they may be Enlightened to some degree, and in some cases even to a very powerful degree – because of undissolved defilements have left a trail of misery, confusion and ignorance in their wake. The last twenty years has been wrought with this kind of confusion. The delicacy of this is beyond measure and it is indeed terrifying to perceive the karmic implications of what it means to claim Enlightenment, for if one would dare to do so, one must indeed be able to manifest and BE that perfection without hesitation and without fear. There is no compromise possible in this, for this indeed is the absolute end of becoming for the individual. Without truly and literally coming to the END and being FINISHED completely with one's ENTIRE history forever, it will be impossible for there not to be some degree of ego influencing the transmission of Enlightenment. That is why it is not a game and it is not a joke. That which is sacred is indeed sacred. No one is exempt from the absolute reckoning of one's entire being. Most of the world-renowned masters, gurus and prophets of our era have left a legacy of, at its worst corruption, and at its least confusion, only for this reason. Before I left him in India the first time, Poonjaji said to me, "You'll be able to do it. No one has been able to do it so far." I didn't know what he meant at the time, but only after several years of teaching did I come to know what is involved and what the stakes truly are.

His reply to my letter was:

> . . . The way you speak in your letter dated July 3rd forced me to believe that there is ONE who speaks my language, has the same Renunciation and Burning FIRE that I have.
> I would never accept if there were a match to me save my great Satguru Ramana who brought me face to face with Light of the SELF. Who said that you speak different than what I do? Only

[your mother] wrote to me that I teach different than what Andrew does. Sometimes I think to send you the copy of her letter to know how even the Mother can be so hard on her own Son and one other man during the Satsang at Haridwar reminded me about the difference. I don't know his or her name for I never care to know who came and who left.

I know that to seek the Truth is just as difficult as to walk on the Razor edge but there is no other way for the Seeker of Truth save this the only WAY. You go your WAY, don't care for the Barking Dogs behind, who would follow you up to their village Limits and return to their own holes. Most of the Americans who came to see me said that they have stayed with Andrew at Totnes or Cambridge or Larkspur and came to India with Andrew's Blessings and always spoke very high of you.

Satguru: Satguru is not a Title that can be conferred by any one to any one. It is a reverential way to address one's Teacher by the student. Even I never use this term for myself nor heard any one addressing me thus. The Maharshi is my Satguru and I address Him thus. To others of course I call them by Indian names because I can not pronounce or remember their names with no other reason and some have requested for the Indian name and I do it. Maybe this helps them not to grab the name and form. . . .

After receiving his letter, I let the matter go.

Some unsettling rumors began to reach me. A meditation teacher who had gone to India to meet Poonjaji, on his return had said publicly that Poonjaji had said Andrew was "off." As Poonjaji had only been extremely supportive of me in letters and in phone calls, I didn't know what to make of it.

Also around this time, I received a letter from one of my students where he related details from a conversation that he had had with my mother while visiting New York. Apparently she had heard that Poonjaji had "skeletons in his closet" – that he had been "womanizing" while travelling and teaching in Europe and had had a child with a young Western student years earlier. I was stunned, but then realized whom this information had come from and concluded that my mother must have made it up in order to discredit Poonjaji, because she, I had been told, disliked him intensely. She had been spending time with the non-teacher teacher U.G. Krishnamurti and related that he felt that Poonjaji was a frustrated would-be world teacher, and he even said that Poonjaji had come to him for advice on how to get a following in America. I felt sickened by my mother's insidious negativity and was upset that she would speak this way about my Guru.

18

As more people began to visit my Guru, more rumors filtered back to me of discontent. The person that had claimed Poonjaji told her to teach was slowly attracting students of mine who had not been able to live up to my teaching. From these people I began to hear things like, "Andrew is corrupting the Dharma," "Andrew is distorting Master Poonjaji's teachings."

Around this time Poonjaji moved to a new house in order to accommodate the growing numbers of people who were coming to see him. I was perplexed to hear several stories of people who had been to see him and who afterwards received letters of glorious praise from him. He would make claim after claim of how rare their meetings had been. I began to wonder what all this could mean, as the effect this seemed to be having was leading people to believe things about themselves that, in my eyes, simply weren't true. As a result, many were becoming overconfident, arrogant and self-satisfied. Suddenly many were claiming "Enlightenment" and I was astounded that a man like Poonjaji, who had set me Free and had so impressed me with his seemingly high standards and intolerance for mediocrity, was now blessing everybody with affirmations of being "finished." I was shocked because I knew very well that Enlightenment is not like an ice cream cone that you can buy at the corner store. It began to seem that with his constant affirmation of almost everyone, the meaning and significance of what Enlightenment truly implies was being cheapened. The true meaning of the event was being distorted and misrepresented. As powerful a teacher as my Guru is, even he does not have the power to finish any and all who come before him.

Coming into the presence of a true Master can and will reveal anyone's *potential* for Enlightenment, and in that seeing, the whole world can and often does turn upside down for a short time. But that vision, which comes from the Grace of the Guru, is usually not the end, but only the beginning. If someone has only realized their potential, and in that they are told that they have come home forever, they have been dangerously misguided into a false sense of freedom. True Freedom must be WON, by each and every individual through their own determination, clear intention and perfect surrender. Grace alone can reveal absolutely everything, but absolutely every-thing – which means the full and immaculate condi-tion of the Awakened state – must be fully accepted, and one who is ready to fully and unconditionally accept the Absolute nature of their own true identity in perfect and unconditional surrender to that alone, is indeed quite rare. Slowly I began to find myself in the midst of quite a predicament where the stakes were very high. I became alarmed. I was in the middle of a public spectacle in which, if I remained absolutely true to what I knew to be true, I would be condemned for it.

One of my students who was travelling in India went to visit Poonjaji. The following is an excerpt from a letter she sent to me:

> ... When I met Poonjaji for the first time, he greeted me very lovingly with his beaming smile

and made me very welcome. I felt great relief and
thought initially everything must be well.
But then the next day a strange thing happened.
When I told him how happy I was to meet my
Grandfather and that I was bringing with me the
love of all your Sangha, his smile weakened and
he made no response. This was very agonizing
and confusing at the time, because I had expected
him to be so happy to meet one of your students
and to ask me all about you and California, but
he had no interest at all. During my time there,
whenever I mentioned your name, he either lost
his smile and turned silent, or quickly changed
the subject. Looking back, the only times he did
speak about you, were when he was making
a point in which he himself was the central
focus. . . .

In November two of my students went to India
to prepare for my arrival in Bodhgaya where I would
be teaching in January. On their way to Bodhgaya
they travelled to Lucknow to visit Poonjaji for a few
days. They brought a letter from me which they hand
delivered to him. In the letter, I told him what had
been occurring around the person he had supposedly
told to teach. I told him I was concerned because she
had told untruths and distortions of the truth regard-
ing myself, and that I was quite concerned about the
confusion that was being caused in his name. I told
him a schism was being created and this was causing
many to doubt my integrity and the purity of my
intention. My students asked to meet with him privately and he agreed. When they presented him with

the letter I had written to him, saying he should read this first, he shouted out loud, "Don't read this – it will pollute your mind!" and explained that he would read it alone as he would be able to "absorb" it. They were shocked and surprised by this. When they tried to speak with him in depth, his responses were confusing. He said that "it is always like this with great men." He said, "The whole world will rise up against a great man and spit. Look at Jesus on the cross, they nailed him, Confucius was poisoned. I'm happy when these things happen. Where there's fire there's smoke." When he was asked, "How can people who claim to love you speak about Andrew this way?" he shook his head and said, "I don't know." Then he said, "I don't know what she's teaching. Tell Andrew to wait and see. The truth will stand alone and truth always prevails." When they told Poonjaji that I didn't know how to respond to the situation because I didn't know where Poonjaji stood, he replied forcefully, "I'm not attached to anyone, I'm not keeping anyone in my heart. Nobody."

19

Poonjaji did not respond to my letter. Worried that I may have offended him, I wrote him a letter on December 7th two weeks before my departure to India.

. . . Please have no doubt that I fully accept my aloneness. I realize that to do that which cannot be done, to know that which cannot be known, and to be able to express the inexpressible, it is absolutely imperative to stand alone. This is the destiny that You have given me and this perfect no-otherness I accept and indeed embrace with open arms, profound gratitude and endless wonder. . . .

We will be leaving for India in two weeks time and we are all very excited about the trip. I am looking very much forward to being with you in Lucknow. . . .

I flew to India with my wife and five of my students where we first stopped in Bombay for three days and stayed with my wife's family. After that we flew to Lucknow to visit Poonjaji for five days before going to Bodhgaya. It was a strange time. Many people were there. The room was full every morning for Satsang and it was the first time I had seen Poonjaji teaching a large group of people. Even though on the surface Poonjaji and his attendants were hospitable and gracious with us, the atmosphere was pervaded with a feeling of mistrust. I assumed that was only due to the fact that several people there had been with me at one time. We had heard that some were complaining that the atmosphere had "changed" when we arrived. I don't know exactly what that could have meant except for the fact that we sat very still, were very quiet and must have seemed "serious." Poonjaji never said a word about me during his Satsang. What was odd was that everybody knew who I was and it seemed that nobody knew exactly where he stood. A former student of mine reported to me that when speaking with Poonjaji about the fact that all of my students would be coming to meet him, he had said, "Why are they coming?"

I wrote to Poonjaji from Bodhgaya:

> . . . We are gathering morning and evening. Over 150 people are here with me and the teachings are flowing out of me endlessly. My demand for total renunciation of ignorance is challenging many who come to see me. Some are ecstatic and some are offended by my confidence, but as each day passes I am only more sure of myself. Father I see again and again that no one dares to Proclaim the True Dharma this way. Father I have no choice – It is pouring out of me. . . .

In another letter I wrote:

> . . . The Fire of Liberation continues to burn brightly inside me. I am constantly overwhelmed and live only to speak about this Realization that You bestowed upon me almost five years ago. Here in Bodhgaya all continues to go very, very well. My formal students are on fire almost as much as I am and my lay students are filled with the excitement and thrill of the Unknown. The Love, Bliss, Joy and Harmony that we are swimming in is always extraordinary, ever new and absolutely intoxicating.
>
> Much controversy is being made here by Your Son amongst the Buddhists from various traditions. A Tibetan Buddhist monk who sat before me in Satsang declared before all the people

gathered that he wanted to give his life to me because he knew instantly upon meeting Your Son that he would attain Enlightenment in this birth!

Yesterday I was invited to meet one of the three highest Tibetan Masters of the Dzog Chen tradition – the Great Perfection teachings. We spoke through an interpreter and he questioned me intensely for half an hour. Many of his students, Tibetan and Western, were present. At the end he confirmed my realization and said I should "please bring countless beings to this Path!"

That Truth that you have revealed to me and the confidence that grows inside of me everyday can't be silent. . . .

Master, we need urgently to discuss these matters for a gulf has begun to appear between Father and Son in the minds of many who come to my Master. This continues to create a difficult situation for your True Son, for a schism has been created, where none should be. This schism continues to grow and causes me deep pain. There is profound disrespect and even contempt from many of my Father's students, and I feel the implications in all this are serious. Father, we need to talk about this together in depth when we meet. . . .

Poonjaji wrote to one of my students during January:

> . . . I am very glad to read your letter giving me details of Dear Andrew's 1st ever appearance at the place of the Buddha, where his teaching had been Lost in the mess of Rituals that He rejected 2500 years ago.

Andrew's Teaching is none other than what the
Buddha had practiced and preached thru his
Sangha.
   I am sure He will help the Seekers after Truth,
to win back Freedom, which is every one's Birth
Right. . . .

A few days later he wrote to my wife:

   . . . I am happy you have kept up your promise to
write to me every other day, about Dear Andrew. . . .
   There is no teacher who can teach as Andrew
is doing. I was confident about his success in helping people who come to Bodhgaya for freedom. . . .
   When you come to Lucknow with your
[students] please intimate and [we] will arrange
special time for you in the evenings or what ever
time that suited. . . .

20

*I*n the midst of the strange atmosphere that pervaded my stay in Lucknow prior to going to Bodhgaya,
a close student of Poonjaji's confirmed some of my
mother's accusations about Master Poonjaji. This
disturbed me. What disturbed me was not that these
things had happened, but that he had asked someone
to lie to me about these matters in order to protect my
idea of who he was. He had ridiculed other teachers
for the same kind of conduct at times, and the obvious hypocrisy in this was troubling.

A week before we left Bodhgaya to go to Lucknow to visit Poonjaji, I had sent a team of students to make all the arrangements for our stay there. They rented enough rooms in two hotels for one hundred and twenty people. Arrangements were made that we would meet together in the conference room of one hotel for three consecutive evenings where meals would be prepared for all. Salt-free meals would also be specially prepared for Poonjaji who had trouble with high blood pressure. All arrangements were made with his approval. It was his suggestion that all of my students come to see him at one time as this would be easier for everybody.

I arrived in Lucknow in the morning. That evening we were all to meet together with Poonjaji. I went straight to his house with a small group of my students to attend his morning Satsang. There were much fewer people there then – about twenty-five. The Satsang lasted for three hours after which we were invited to stay for lunch. After lunch when I inquired as to what time he wanted to be picked up in the evening, he shook his head and said, "I'm too tired. If I come it'll kill me." My heart sank. I said, "OK, Master."

Everybody had been looking so much forward to meeting him. In the minds of all my students he was their benevolent grandfather – the God-man who had set me Free. They all loved him without question and felt a profound intimacy with him through my constant reference to him as the source of my Self. When I went back to the hotel, I told everyone that he was not feeling well and that we would meet the following day. The next morning I returned to his house to attend his morning Satsang with a small group of my students. Again it lasted for about three hours. After lunch when I asked him what time he wanted to be picked up in the evening, he looked at me and said, "I can't come tonight." He continued, "Chandrashekhar [the Prime Minister of India] is in town and will be giving a public talk near your hotel. There will be a big crowd and lots of police there." I knew this wasn't true. Then he picked up that day's newspaper and handed it to one of his attendants telling him to look inside, saying he would find reference to it there. He did not. I knew Poonjaji was lying. I went outside and asked my wife and another very close student of mine to appeal to him. I hoped that they might be able to convince him to come. When they did try and appeal to him, he responded forcefully saying, "I'm not coming!" They were both taken aback by the intensity of his response. They continued to try and convince him to come, telling him how much everybody loved him and how much they were looking forward to seeing him. Hearing this, he softened a little bit and started to ask a few questions about what floor our rooms were on, and said that maybe the following day he would come. When they tried to get him to fix a time, he would not.

On leaving, I asked his closest attendant to step outside and speak with me. When I asked him what was going on, he responded by trying to tell me that "this was good for me," implying that this was some kind of lesson or teaching. I said, "What am I supposed to learn from this? I have one hundred and twenty people waiting to meet my Guru. What am I supposed to tell them?" Then I said, "The only reason he doesn't want to come is because these people have nothing to do with him – that's why." Reluctantly he agreed.

Walking away I knew it was over. I knew I was alone.

REVELATION

21

 *T*hat afternoon I met with my formal students,
which was a little more than half the group, and told
them what had happened. We decided together not
to accept this disrespectful and ungracious behavior
from Master Poonjaji, and it was agreed that the
group would go together to his house with all the
gifts and garlands that they had prepared late that
afternoon. I didn't go, but waited at the hotel for
them to return. When they arrived he was out for
a walk with his attendants. When he came back he
invited everybody inside. My students met his reti-
cence with enthusiasm and his indifference with love.
One after the other, they would approach him, prostrate at his feet, garland him and thank him. Mean-
while some effusively told him how much love they
felt for him. In spite of this, he appeared uneasy and
seemed to be struggling in a situation which was out
of his control. My students only came to love him and
extend their gratitude. Nobody wanted anything
from him. He didn't know how to respond. Except
for brief moments when he seemed to genuinely
enjoy everybody's company, for the most part he
wavered between what looked like reluctant joy and
simple tolerance. What struck everyone the most was

that he seemed unable to relate to them as finders. Whenever he would address anyone, he would speak to them as if they were still seeking for something.

He didn't come the next day. Over the next two mornings, I divided the rest of the group that was with me in half and together we went to his morning Satsangs. As the majority of these people were not formal members of my Sangha, they were for the most part uninformed about the drama that had been unfolding. I brought as many of my formal students as could squeeze in, as they very much wanted to be able to see Poonjaji teaching. Quite unexpectedly, on both days they asked him questions on a topic that we had been speaking about: how is it that supposedly Enlightened teachers can, in spite of their Enlightenment, behave in unenlightened ways? This question was asked a few times by different people as they were obviously not satisfied with his responses. He seemed to find these questions annoying and became very serious. He said, "This has nothing to do with Enlightenment, this is only religion." And finally he said, "Don't judge a teacher by what they do, only by what they say." My mouth dropped open. Then quite uncharacteristically, he abruptly ended the Satsang and said, "Let's take a picture."

One afternoon I asked to meet with Poonjaji privately and he agreed, telling me to come back later in the day. I arrived in the early evening and we spent two hours together. His attendants went out for a walk, so we were completely alone. We both sat on a mattress on the floor. He sat leaning his back on the wall with his legs crossed in front of him. I sat very close, facing him directly, often with my hands on his knees. Initially I asked him if there was anything at all about me that he was unhappy with. He responded without hesitation, saying that he was "completely satisfied" with me. He went on to tell me how pleased he was to meet my students and how impressed he had been with them. I then explained to him much of what I had already written to him about. I told him of the agony I had been feeling about the gulf that had arisen between us in the minds of many of his students, to which he responded, "I don't have any students!" I continued to say that I was concerned about his legacy. He had handed over his robe to me, and because of this I was disturbed by the antagonism and disrespect coming from many of his devotees – especially from those whom he had encouraged to teach. He told me that he was also disturbed by this. He said, "Yes, then they can't learn from you." Then he asked me, "What should I do? Tell me what I should do." I said, "Master, you have to make things clear." Then he responded in a way that was unexpected. He said, while putting his hand on my leg, "Andrew, you mustn't have this pain – it's *my* responsibility, I'll take care of it. We don't have to talk anymore about this. OK?" I said, "OK." There was a sense of profound intimacy between us and a genuine warmth that had not been there for a long time. In the cab on the way back to the hotel I felt a sense of relief, but deeply was unconvinced. I was skeptical about what the future would bring.

The last morning I was in Lucknow, I went to his Satsang with a small group of my students. When one of them went up to him to say good-bye, he asked her, "Are you my granddaughter or my daughter? Which is it?"

22

*A*fter Lucknow I went to Kathmandu for a month where I spent some time teaching. The high point of my time there was a second meeting that I had with the Tibetan Rimpoche whom I had met in Bodhgaya. When I told him that because of my doubtlessness and my relatively young age, many found my confidence threatening and hard to accept, he responded saying that all Enlightened people have the same problem. He said that the Buddha had many heretics that were making a lot of trouble for him and even mentioned that Jesus was hung on the cross because people felt threatened by him. When I spoke about the delicacy of the Teaching, he said the most important thing is that if I had absolutely no doubt, then that was enough. There was nothing else that I needed. He went on to say, "Everybody will think what they want anyway, even if the Buddha was in front of them." He continued to explain that there were different kinds of sentient beings and because of obscurations many would not see him as Enlightened. We spent a few hours together and had a fascinating talk discussing different aspects of the Teaching. We covered many topics such as the necessity for renunciation in the spiritual life, the relationship of thought and karma, how precious was the jewel of Enlightenment and how rare it was to find a person who could truly receive the Teaching.

On my way back to California I travelled with a small group of my students. We spent three days on a beautiful island in Malaysia followed by two days in Hong Kong. I arrived back in the middle of March.

About a month after my return from Asia, I was shocked to learn that the person who Poonjaji would not confirm that he had asked to teach had said in a public gathering: "Andrew has a serious misunderstanding. Those who have been hurt by Andrew should come to speak with me or fly directly to see Poonjaji, they need not write." When I found out this was happening apparently under my Guru's specific instructions, I was horrified. I went to Seattle to teach for three weeks and when I returned, I asked one of my close students to call one of Poonjaji's intimate disciples to ask him what was going on. My worst fears were confirmed. But more than this, it became obvious why such a gulf had arisen between my Master and myself. It was finally clear beyond the human drama of suspicion, betrayal or competition that we disagreed on the most fundamental principles.

Hearing Poonjaji's disciple's understanding of what Enlightenment was and was not – based on his intimate involvement with my Guru – revealed in a shocking way to me that what I understood and what he understood were very, very different. I now knew why my Master and many of his devotees disagreed so strongly with my teaching. I realized that what I had suspected for some time now was true – I had a completely different "view" of Enlightenment. What I was teaching and what my Master was teaching were diametrically opposed to each other. Hearing some of the things one of his closest disciples had said about Enlightenment revealed to me that I had obviously surpassed my own Teacher, and it was because of this that the harmony and ability for true and profound communication had ceased.

His disciple had said that in Enlightenment things didn't have to make sense. He said that oneness had nothing to do with what happens here and is beyond manifestation on this planet. Apparently he didn't believe that it was possible to come to the end of self-centered behavior. He said that in Poonjaji's teaching there is acceptance of the ego and that in my teaching there wasn't space for the ego. He said that Poonjaji acted out of ego and that he and others had observed this. What they concluded from this was that ego never ceases, no matter how Enlightened a person may be. He said that after Enlightenment there are still very strong "tendencies" that have to come out in order to "burn themselves out," and that they will not create karma for the Enlightened person, because being Enlightened they will be free from the consequences of their own actions! He said their actions will only have effects on other people. His main point was that Enlightenment is freedom from identification with one's actions. Hearing this appalled me, but at least it made clear what the problem had been all along. This kind of thinking and this kind of teaching was and is the most dangerous and profoundly deluded misunderstanding of the teaching of Enlightenment. It means "I'm free so I can do whatever I want." How many gurus have gotten away with murder using this as a justification for doing whatever they felt like doing? The whole point of Enlightenment is to be Awake to such a degree that one will *not* create karma any longer, and ultimately should be the end of karma altogether. My definition of this has always been no longer causing suffering to others as a result of acting out of ignorance.

I have always insisted that if a person claims they want to be Free, it is imperative that they cease to create the kind of suffering for self and other that results from identification with ignorance. Poonjaji apparently was concerned that I had "hurt" people because some of my students had come to him with wounded pride. Facing the truth about oneself is not always easy. Those who aren't willing to face the truth as it is, which means facing the reality of their own condition as it is, may feel wounded when they find they are unwilling to do so, but the only wound will be to their pride. To come to the condition of being fully Awake means that pride and the one who is proud have died forever in the perfect knowledge of their own true identity. This man didn't believe that it was possible that the expression of ego – which *is* pride – could come to an end. If it were not possible for the expression of ego to come to an end, then what could the significance of Enlightenment possibly be? What was I to do with this? What was I to think? This was madness!

Beyond the clear understanding of what our philosophical differences were, I was deeply pained to find out that my Guru was speaking against me to others while at the same time actively deceiving me as to how he honestly felt. Those who were coming back from visits with him knew more about how he felt about me than I did. This was unbearable. When a student of mine, who had been unable to live up to his own proclamations of absolute interest in Free-dom alone and had been disrespectful to myself and my students, went to see Poonjaji, he was given the name "Sher" which means lion. I concluded that Poonjaji must have given him the name "lion" be-cause in Poonjaji's eyes he had the courage to stand up to me. Apparently Poonjaji wrote to this man saying that the person who told this man about him was a sheep and would always be a sheep. That person was myself. Poonjaji had said in one of his Satsangs, "The only mistake the Buddha ever made was having a Sangha." He also said that "Sangha is for sheep." He had a profound aversion to any kind of form or structure and never had the courage to speak to me about this. I had written to him many times explaining to him how extraordinary was the explosion of love, intimacy and most importantly *evolution* that was the "form" that had spontaneously arisen around me. He had always replied only expressing wonder, amazement and joy at, to use his word, the "miracle" that was happening around his son. What disturbed me the most was that he didn't want to know the truth. When I had brought all of my students to meet him and he had had the opportunity to spend time in their company in order to find out if any doubts he may have had were valid, he didn't take it. His extreme disinterest proved that he obviously had no desire to find out. But even more than that, he seemed very interested in hearing about tales of wounded pride, and apparently even believed and was speaking about a story in which I was accused of accepting money from someone and not returning it. Even those close to him who were profoundly critical of myself and my teachings were surprised that he would believe this. I asked myself again and again, what is he doing? I felt betrayed beyond measure and horrified at the lengths to which he seemed to be going to undermine me. His disciple who was now teaching in his name inquired how to contact people around me who may be thinking of leaving. Another disciple was his contact person in California, looking out for those supposedly "hurt" by me. Later, he even asked a man visiting him in Lucknow who had been my student to call his ex-wife, a very close student of mine, and tell her "to come right away." This made it even more obvious that there was a lot more going on than mere philosophical disagreement.

In June I went to England where I taught for three weeks. From London I wrote Poonjaji the following letter:

> . . . Master, I feel compelled to write to you about the gulf that is growing between us. Many things have happened and are continuing to happen that cause me great pain and anguish. I wrote you several letters about these matters to which you did not reply. My students spoke with you directly about these matters and I also spoke with you privately in Lucknow last February. I must admit I am very confused by much of what is taking place around my Master. Recently while I was in California, two of your devotees came to me on separate occasions after having requested a meeting with me. They both behaved very badly. I am not used to being spoken to by anyone with such aggressive disrespect and arrogance. They both told me that their Master was shedding tears of displeasure about the conduct of Andrew and demanded to know what my response was. From them and others who have been to see you I hear again and again the same thing: "Master Poonjaji is upset with Andrew, Master Poonjaji disagrees with Andrew's teaching," etc., etc. Almost

without exception all the people I hear about who come back from seeing you are saying these things and also almost without exception speak with disdain and disrespect about myself and my students. In addition to this, your disciple who has been teaching in the San Francisco area, apparently under your specific instructions, has been saying publicly that Master Poonjaji says that all those who have been hurt by Andrew can fly to see him, they need not write first. She is saying, "Andrew has a serious misunderstanding." As your reputation is growing, many who have never even met me are hearing these things and are doubting me because of this. My close student, whom you met last year on several occasions, spoke at length with one of your intimate devotees about these matters and he confirmed that Master Poonjaji disagrees with Andrew's teachings and speaks openly about this. He said that Master Poonjaji was very disturbed about stories he hears about Andrew. He even said Master Poonjaji believes that Andrew had taken money from someone and would not give it back, and if Andrew went on like this he would become like Rajneesh. . . .

Dear Father, how could all these things be true? It breaks my heart that you would speak against me in this way and it breaks my heart that you could have such serious doubts about my integrity.

He also said to my student that Andrew cannot tolerate being criticized. This is clearly ridiculous and untrue. I have no objection to criticism and I have come to expect it because I have realized ever since I began teaching over five years ago that few have the courage to meet me in truth. My passion and integrity have been called arrogance for over five years and this does not trouble me at all. But what I find unbearable and unthinkable is that my own Guru could doubt me and speak out against me in this way. For a long time now I could never understand how and why almost all my Master's devotees, save very few, were suspicious and even contemptuous of me. It was only after his confirmation that my worst fears became a reality and I was forced to bear the unbearable weight and burden that this revelation is to me. Master, I can't begin to tell you how much this hurts me and causes me to suffer. At the present time, as a result of all this, a public spectacle is taking place. For me this is a living nightmare the likes of which I never could have imagined five years ago when you slapped me on the back and shouted in my ear, "HAVE IT!"

I was shocked last February when it became obvious to me that you had no interest in spending time with my students who had all come to Lucknow only to love you and to pay their respects to you. If you had serious questions and doubts about my teaching, I can't understand why you didn't want to make the effort to spend time with those people who have not come to you from me with wounded pride but who came with hearts bursting with love, joy and confidence. My students were shocked and dumbfounded to hear the stories that they were afraid and lived in fear. When they heard this, they all burst out laughing and shook their heads in disbelief. Master, you yourself said that to walk this path is like walking on the razor's edge. Master, you know as well as I do that not everybody has the courage to know the truth or to live the truth. I have never betrayed anyone since I have been teaching and I have only dearly loved and energetically encouraged and instructed all who have come to me to live a life of freedom and truth. Some are unable and unwilling to do this. To those people I cannot and will not lie. If they are dishonest and hypocritical and betray their own heart, I will not tell them that they are not doing that. For this and this alone I am criticized. Without truth there can be no lasting liberation. Without integrity there can be no real love. If I am accused by many of insisting that people rise up out of the mess of self-deception, I plead guilty. But my Master, I repeat I have NEVER betrayed a soul. If my insistence that people should cease to deceive themselves causes them to turn against me, what should I do? What can I do? I am helpless only before those whose desire for freedom is not genuine. . . . Why are you blaming me if some get hurt? This is unavoidable, the condition of humanity being what it is. You yourself have explained this to me in detail many times.

Your devotee said, "Master Poonjaji will never interfere with what Andrew is doing because that would interfere with Andrew's freedom." Master, the public spectacle that is taking place this very minute has created a cloud of doubt and suspicion about your own son. You knew when you sent me off to Rishikesh that the consequences of our meeting were vast and unthinkable. . . . Master, it is no surprise that the world is not ready for one such as me. I know that the power of the truth that comes out of me frightens many, but it is only their own hypocrisy and self-deception that is being challenged. The passion I feel and the passion that comes through me I cannot control. You knew the meaning of all this much better than myself. The revolution that you proclaimed is occurring. For people to trust the unthinkable nature of my call it is hard enough, but with the FATHER standing against the SON, it is making my extraordinary task much more difficult and also undermining many people's faith in me. This is unbearable to me and is extraordinarily difficult for me to accept.

Father, why hast thou forsaken me?

He never responded.

23

In July I travelled from England to Holland where I taught for three weeks in Amsterdam. While there, I unexpectedly met a man who had been my Guru's disciple eighteen years earlier. We spent an afternoon together and he told me the story of his time with Poonjaji. Under the circumstances, the meeting almost seemed predestined as it served to be an absolute confirmation of my own experience with my Guru – and more. This man had been Poonjaji's disciple for three years. He first met Poonjaji in Barcelona. At the time, he was involved with a Dharma group there and they invited Poonjaji back to Barcelona to teach. He said that while he was with Poonjaji, he was his "right hand man" and that Poonjaji called him his "chosen son." He said Poonjaji wanted to have a center in Barcelona that would serve as a headquarters for Europe and America. Poonjaji said that his energy would stream through this man's eyes, and chose him to be the head of his "center for the West." He said without hesitation that Poonjaji was a "megalomaniac" with aspirations to become a world teacher. Apparently Poonjaji's ambition pushed this man and others towards this end. He described several incidents in which people had been overwhelmed by Poonjaji's intensity, even to the point of having nervous breakdowns, and said Poonjaji seemed not to care at all about the mess he was leaving in his wake. He further confirmed the fact of Poonjaji's promiscuity and described how Poonjaji often lied, talked behind people's backs, distorted stories that people told him and played people against each other. He said that Poonjaji only cared about himself and often misused his power as a Guru for his own benefit. When I described to him my own experience of the last few years he replied, "Of course, that's normal. He's competitive and jealous." After spending time with Poonjaji in India and observing the same kind of duplicity and, what he called "slander" in Poonjaji's relationships, he broke off his association with him. He wrote to all the people who had met Poonjaji through him in Spain and France telling them about his conduct, and apparently as a result of this, all of Poonjaji's students in Spain left Poonjaji. He said he was quite ill after leaving Poonjaji and that it took him several months to recover what he called his "integrity." In spite of his denials to the contrary, it seemed to me that he was still quite upset about it.

24

 W hen I had first met my Guru, the majority of the time that we spent together we were alone. As I said earlier, I was impressed with his boldness, his outrageous absolute conviction and his seeming intolerance for hypocrisy and mediocrity. For this I respected him deeply, and in light of this was very surprised to find that he was a man of many faces. When I had asked him what his opinion was of the now famous deceased Guru Neem Karoli Baba, he went on to describe in detail about how he had met him and that he knew that he was completely insane and "mad," but that many people mistook his insanity for Enlightenment. One of my students who spent a few days alone with him reported having the same discussion with him. Several years later, after my book had come out and he was gradually becoming more well-known, when devotees of Neem Karoli would go to him he would praise him as the highest.

My absolute insistence for the Truth alone was, it seemed, the very essence of the schism. It seemed that in this I was going too far even for him, for in my reflection, his own hypocrisy and duplicity were brought into the light. No wonder he had objection to my teaching! He had said about six months after I had met him in front of a small group of people while I was there, "I see a tornado in his eyes and it disturbs me!" He said this with the most serious look imaginable, and at the time, I honestly had no idea what he was referring to in me. Shortly after one of his devotees heard from one of my students that Poonjaji's past was not stainless, another of my students received a letter from Poonjaji's intimate circle saying, "[Andrew's] mere footprint will make Mother Earth weep" and it would be "sinful to see the face of the one who behaves this way." The letter also said that my students were "like erring ghosts neither alive nor dead." As I suspected, I was soon told that my Guru had been involved in the writing of this letter. Shortly after that I heard that he had said, "I can make a thousand Andrews, but he can't make one Poonjaji."

FINAL LIBERATION

25

Whatis Enlightenment? What is Enlightenment?
What is Enlightenment? This is the question that has
been plaguing me and thoroughly preoccupying me
day and night. At first, as can well be imagined, I was
attached to the fairy tale that the initial meeting with
my Guru had been. A story made in heaven, truly out
of this world, perfect in its ecstatic love and profound
and intimate union. The FACT of the result of our
meeting has never changed. This fact – the explosion
of revelation and insight unimaginable in all its glory
– has never left me. For almost six years, I have been
thoroughly immersed and absolutely drowned, drunk
in the full and perfect knowledge of my own true
identity. What does this mean? What does this *really*
mean to me? It means that without fail I have always
been able to see clearly when it has been necessary to
do so. In this seeing I am never alone. The mystery of
separation, which is duality that pretends to create
the illusion of ignorance and bondage, has been destroyed forever. How to describe what it is to know
the Truth? How to describe what it is to see clearly
with vision unobscured, immaculate in its perfect
reflection of the Real?

When so few truly want to see, what is one who is able to see to do? For almost six years now, I have been faced with the fact that the depth and clarity of my vision is for many simply too much. And yet – my inspiration never wanes! It seems that the greater is the resistance to my heart, the more passionate I feel about expressing the Truth clearly and accurately. What it is that runs through my veins, that sets my heart on fire, that lights up my whole nervous system *wants* the Truth to be known. I am unafraid only because I know that what I am seeing *is* the Truth. I feel safe in the knowledge that my mind has been destroyed – it has been destroyed in the knowledge of the Truth itself. How dare I say this? Because it is true. Every day that passes only serves to confirm that fact again and again and again. When someone dares to see through my eyes, the revelation that is the instantaneous chain reaction is extraordinary beyond measure. The mind is consumed in that knowledge that the heart always knows, and that perfection reveals all unceasingly. It is ever new! Ever new! If one has truly woken up, one can never take a position in this knowledge, for it is beyond any position that could ever be taken by anyone. At the same time, the greater the depth that one has come to in this full and perfect understanding, the more profound will be the stand that one *has* to take here and now in this world of time and space. What is Enlightenment? What is Enlightenment? Depth of true insight into this ungraspable mystery is always perfectly revealed in time and in space. It is *that* that I have come to understand.

I was attached to the fairy tale. A year and a half ago when it began to become apparent that there was obviously a discrepancy between the way I was seeing and the way my Guru was seeing, I was forced to look again. Look again I did. And again and again and again. To be honest, I have never stopped looking. I have always had this passion burning inside me to know what is true. For some reason that I don't know, I could never be satisfied with vague inconsistencies. I always wanted to know. There was always something very unsettling about relative confusion. The Absolute Truth itself, alone and untouched, is beyond confusion or clarity. But the world of illusion, time and space is very well within the reach and grasp of any mortal man to understand if they would dare to leave everything behind in the quest for that perfect jewel of Enlightenment. In that jewel, in its reflection all is revealed perfectly. All shades of lightness and darkness, depth, width and breadth are all seen AS THEY ARE. That is the secret! That is the mystery and that is the source of the true joy that Liberates and that is Freedom itself.

For a long time now I have been asking myself the question: what is the relationship between conduct and knowledge, between realization and action, between experience and transformation? After my initial meeting with my Guru when those who came into contact with me began to spontaneously

Awaken, I assumed that we would naturally meet together in this Absolute and Perfect understanding. Usually we did, but I began to notice very quickly that the depth and breadth of this meeting would often begin to show and express limitation sooner or later. I began to realize that the weight of karma, which for some miraculous reason had fallen off my shoulders forever, had not and would not so easily fall away in the conceptual framework of most individuals. In spite of profound Awakening, so much remained still obscured. The light that had been revealed was not FULLY able to express itself absolutely and without any trace of obscuration. Hindrances still seemed to remain, sometimes gross and sometimes subtle. Slowly but surely I began to realize that the whole question of Awakening is infinite in its subtlety and complexity. I began to see more and more clearly how delicate it all is, how powerful is the conditioning and how difficult indeed it is to let go to the degree that not even a speck of dust is left to obscure or corrupt the perfect purity of the light itself.

Initially I could not understand how those who had been so deeply affected by me could betray that most Perfect and Absolute knowledge that had been naturally and effortlessly revealed to them. But eventually I began to see that with the weight of karma and the tremendous momentum that it accrues in time, it is indeed *very* easy to understand how THAT can be betrayed. How? By the sheer weight of the influence of memory. The memory I'm speaking about goes way beyond this life alone. There is far too much involved in this kind of process for one lifetime alone. I've seen how the influence of one THOUGHT can so easily, and usually imperceptibly, instantly become TWENTY YEARS OF A HUMAN LIFE. The influence of one thought can easily and often does become an ENTIRE human life. The power of discrimination necessary to cut through any and all thought to see directly as the Source, perfectly unobscured, is literally unimaginable. It is so delicate! Human beings are so fragile, so easily distracted and so weak in their faith. So much encouragement is needed to simply REMEMBER the possibility.

It was after deep scrutiny of the fact that those who had tasted deeply the truth of their own Self-nature could mechanically turn their backs on that, that I realized that those who not only had tasted deeply, but had BECOME THAT, were also capable of the same kind of betrayal. But there was a difference. The ones who had only tasted deeply could never claim OWNERSHIP. Those who had BECOME that HAD claimed ownership. They WERE that. They MANIFESTED that. It was who they were. It reflected itself as themselves. They were Enlightened and they could speak clearly, eloquently and passionately about THAT to such a degree that people would, in their company, even realize that themselves to some degree. The point is that IN SPITE OF EXTRAORDINARY REALIZATION, the influence and weight of karma can and usually does remain to some degree.

To what degree? To the degree that that individual is able to create suffering for themselves and others due to ignorant actions motivated by selfish desires. The range of influence can go from the gross to a degree of subtlety almost imperceptible. How many have realized that immaculate condition to such a degree that it remains immaculate, untouched forever and ever again? Very few.

I have looked and pondered often and at great length about how and why over the last twenty or thirty years almost all of the modern masters, gurus and prophets have to some degree or other failed. Many of them were and are Enlightened to an extraordinary degree – to an unusual degree. But in spite of that why have they failed? Why do I say they have failed? Because the degree of cynicism in this day and age about the possibility of perfection, the realization of perfection, the manifestation of perfection and the expression of perfection is extraordinary to say the least. Most people who claim to be interested in Truth and Enlightenment, deeply don't really believe that it's possible to realize perfect goodness to the degree that it can be manifested and expressed consistently and without error. Why is that? It is only because those who claimed to have fully arrived simply had not come all the way home – because in spite of their unusual and extraordinary Enlightenment, the trail left by most has been less than perfect, and usually marred with some degree of confusion, hypocrisy, and in more cases than not, even deceit.

The one who would claim Enlightenment in this birth and who would also dare to show the way for others must be able to BE a reflection of that purity to an extraordinary degree. There must be the attainment of perfect consistency of goodness, selflessness and the demonstration of that PURE INTENTION that wants only itself and NOTHING ELSE. Without that attainment and the perfection of that attainment, the consistency I'm speaking about will not be there. It is the inconsistency in the expression of perfect goodness that has created the most extraordinary depth of confusion, misunderstanding and outright foolishness in the name of Enlightenment. How is it possible for a man like Bhagwan Rajneesh to inspire hundreds of thousands of people to abandon the world in the name of Truth and Freedom to a degree unmatched in modern times, and yet at the same time leave behind him a legacy of confusion and misunderstanding equally unparalleled in the sheer numbers which he influenced? How is it that someone like Chögyam Trungpa, who through the power of his understanding and extraordinary mind was able to do so much and influence so many in bringing the Buddha Dharma to the West, leave behind him such an outrageous mess of gross self-indulgence, drunkenness and even death? How is it that someone so perfect, so beautiful, so utterly pure as the great J. Krishnamurti, who literally throughout his long life influenced millions with his passionate plea to awaken from the dream of selfishness and delusion, ultimately have so little effect? How could a spiritual genius and profoundly Awakened man like Da Free John, who makes such a mockery of his own genius through his painfully obvious megalomaniacal rantings, leave so many lost and confused? And how is it that his teacher, the Guru of gurus, the extraordinarily powerful Swami Muktananda, who literally jolted so many thousands far beyond what they imagined possible, leave behind him so much skepticism and doubt as to the actual depth and degree of his attainment? How is all this possible? How could so many be left in such confusion in the wake of these examples?

It's possible because almost no one dares to be sure what the Truth actually is. If there is ever going to be any real change, which means a true flowering of Real Awakening, then some individuals have got to have the courage to look deeply enough to find out for themselves what the Truth actually is. I always say that if an individual wants to be Free, then there is no one in this world who will be able to stop them. The necessity for absolute discrimination and un- bridled passion in and for the pursuit and discovery of the Truth alone is extraordinary. So few seem to have the willingness to abandon absolutely every and all thought formation and subtle concept in the pur- suit of that Perfect understanding. It is so easy to get stuck even in imperfect Enlightenment. It may indeed be that one's very life, as one has known it, may need to be questioned in its every aspect to such an extraor- dinary degree that it may literally dissolve into emptiness before one's very eyes – if one truly wants to go ALL THE WAY. How many are willing? How many truly want to know? Who is willing to pay the price? There is more involved than just surrender or even very good intentions. The absolute responsibility necessary for the pursuit and attainment of Perfect understanding is indeed terrifying even to conceive. In this kind of absolute responsibility, one literally stands alone in the unknown and dares to KNOW. But I am not speaking of only peeking at or glimpsing that Perfection. I am speaking about going so far as having the courage to literally claim responsibility for that Perfection. It is then and only then that a human being will be able to bring all doubt, fear, confusion and cynicism to an end in a way that will truly have significance.

August 1973, at seventeen just before returning to the U.S. to enter music school.

1982, a year before my first trip to India.

Puri, March 1984.

*April 1986, towards the end of my first
meeting with Poonjaji.*

"The Fairy Tale" - September 1986.

Walking with my mother in Rishikesh, June 1986.

Dharamsala, August 1986.

With students in Florence, Italy, March 1987.

*Devon, October 1986. Shortly
after I began teaching in England.*

Teaching in Cambridge, Massachusetts, December 1988.

Picnicking in Boulder, Colorado, spring 1990.

San Francisco Bay, Guru Purnima Day 1990.

On a walk with students in Tennessee Valley, California, 1990.

Arriving in Bodhgaya, January 1991.

With my wife on my birthday, October 1990.

Picnic on Angel Island,
Guru Purnima Day 1990.

Last visit, December 1990.

Lucknow, December 1990.

Teaching in Bodhgaya, January 1991.

With students in Kathmandu, February 1991.

Returning from Asia, March 1991.

Victory in Amsterdam, July 199

Also by Andrew Cohen

Enlightenment is a Secret